GILLS (lamellae)

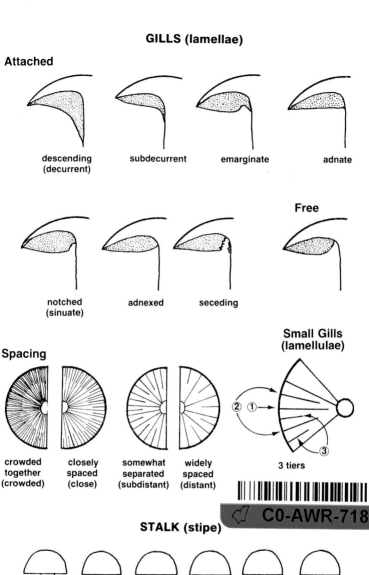

Attached

descending (decurrent)   subdecurrent   emarginate   adnate

Free

notched (sinuate)   adnexed   seceding   adnate

Spacing

crowded together (crowded)   closely spaced (close)   somewhat separated (subdistant)   widely spaced (distant)

Small Gills (lamellulae)

3 tiers

STALK (stipe)

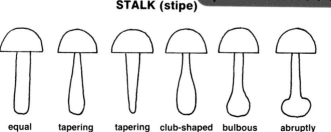

equal   tapering above   tapering below   club-shaped (clavate)   bulbous   abruptly bulbous

The Macmillan Field Guide Series includes

Birds of North America: Eastern Region

Astronomy: A Step-by-Step Guide to the Night Sky

Rocks and Minerals

Wildflowers

Fossils

Weather and Forecasting

Mushrooms

Trees

Birds of North America: Western Region (forthcoming)

MACMILLAN FIELD GUIDES

MUSHROOMS

A Quick Reference Guide to Mushrooms of North America

by

Alan Bessette
and
Walter J. Sundberg

COLLIER BOOKS
Macmillan Publishing Company, New York
Collier Macmillan Publishers, London

On the cover: Scarlet Waxy Cap, *Hygrophorus coccineus* (page 134).
Photograph by Alan Bessette.

Copyright © 1987 by Macmillan Publishing Company,
a division of Macmillan, Inc.

Macmillan Publishing Company
866 Third Avenue, New York, N.Y. 10022
Collier Macmillan Canada, Inc.

Library of Congress Cataloging-in-Publication Data

Bessette, Alan.
   Mushrooms: a quick reference guide to mushrooms
of North America.

   (Macmillan field guides)
   Bibliography: p.
   Includes index.
   1. Mushrooms—North American—Identification.
I. Sundberg, Walter J.   II. Title.   III. Series.
QK617.B48 1987   589.2'097   87-11718

ISBN 0-02-063690-3

10   9   8   7   6   5   4   3   2   1

The Macmillan Field Guide Series: Mushrooms is also published
in a hardcover edition by Macmillan Publishing Company.

Printed in the United States of America

Table of Contents

Acknowledgments

Several people have helped to make this field guide possible. We thank Linda Neuman for her technical assistance. Diana Bessette and Janet Sundberg read portions of the manuscript, made valuable suggestions, and also provided some technical assistance. We are grateful to Catherine Ardrey, David Arora, Fredda Burton, Richard L. Homola, Gregory Mueller, John A. Richardson, Donald M. Simons, Betty Strack, and Harry D. Thiers for contributing slides that improved the photographic quality of this work, and to Geoffrey Kibby for his excellent drawings. We especially thank Mike Agnes at Macmillan for his guidance and creativity and for giving us the opportunity to write the book. We wish to express our indebtedness to all mycologists—past and present, professional and amateur alike; it is their research that has made our task easier. Lastly, we acknowledge Harry D. Thiers and Richard L. Homola for introducing us to the wondrous world of mushrooms and for their never-ending inspiration and encouragement.

Alan Bessette
Walter J. Sundberg

Introduction

Fungi and Mushrooms

Mushrooms are just one example of a large and highly diverse group of organisms called fungi. The kingdom Fungi includes molds and mildews, yeasts, rusts and smuts, mushrooms, bracket fungi, and many other forms. Fungi are similar in many ways to plants; unlike plants, however, they lack the green pigment chlorophyll. Thus, they cannot produce their own food through the process of photosynthesis, using sunlight, water, and carbon dioxide. Instead, they obtain their food by breaking down dead organic matter and thus play a vital role in the ecological process of nutrient recycling. In some cases they obtain food by attacking and living on or within other living plants or, more rarely, animals or even other fungi (as parasites).

The vegetative body of a fungus consists of a large number of microscopic, branching, tubular threads called hyphae. An entire mass of hyphae is known as a mycelium. The hyphae grow on or permeate a food source (known as the substrate), such as a decomposing log, decaying leaves, or dung. The white or sometimes colored mycelium can often be seen growing on the underside of fallen logs and branches or binding together partially decomposed leaves and other debris in the lower levels of forest litter. As they grow, the hyphae produce digestive enzymes that are secreted into the substrate, to break down its complex structure into simpler substances that can be absorbed and used by the fungus as food.

Under appropriate conditions, actively growing hyphae (primary mycelium) or, in some cases, other specialized structures can fuse, initiating the process of reproduction. In some fungi, such as the cup fungi and morels, this fusion leads directly to culmination of the reproductive process described below. In others, such as the true mushrooms, the fused hyphae can continue to grow, forming new hyphae (secondary mycelium) that often persist in the substrate for years, reproducing intermittently.

When sufficient mycelium growth and nutrient accumulation have occurred and when environmental conditions are favorable, the mycelium of those species referred to as fleshy fungi produces characteristic fleshy fruiting bodies. These are the visible parts of many familiar fungi, such as mushrooms, morels, shelf fungi, and puffballs. The fruiting bodies are highly structured aggregations of hyphae that are modified for the production and dispersal of their reproductive cells called spores. Fruiting bodies are thus at least crudely analogous to apples on an apple tree. With some species, fruiting bodies may be produced at almost any time of year. With others, such as the morels, fruiting may be restricted to a distinctly seasonal, and often relatively short, period.

The mature spores of most species are released into the air and, because of their very small size and light weight, are carried far and wide by the wind. However, some fleshy fungi have developed other means of spore dispersal. For example, the bird's nest fungi, also known as fairy cups, form their spores in small packets (the "eggs") held within a cup-like fruiting body (the "nest"). The force created by water falling or dripping into the cup throws the "eggs" and their spores some distance away. The fungi known as stinkhorns, on the other hand, form their spores in a foul-smelling slime that attracts flies. As they walk over and eat the odoriferous mass, the flies ingest some spores; other spores stick to their hairs and legs. Spores are thus carried off and later are dislodged or deposited in the flies' feces. Still other fungi, like truffles and false truffles, which grow underground, rely heavily for spore dispersal on the activity of mice, squirrels, and other small mammals that eat them and deposit the spores in their droppings. Regardless of its mode of dispersal, if a spore lands in a location with a suitable environment (temperature, moisture, for nutrition, etc.), it will germinate to form a new hypha, which in turn will grow, branch, and form a new primary mycelium.

Some species of fungi, especially many of the mushrooms, form an intricate and mutually beneficial relationship, called a mycorrhizal association, with the roots of living trees and other plants. Some mycorrhizal fungi grow in association with only one tree species; others are less restricted. The mycorrhizal association is of nutritional benefit to the fungus; it also increases the potential uptake of nutrients from the soil by the tree roots. Thus, it is very significant in the maintenance and growth of forest vegetation.

How to Use This Guide

The species illustrated are arranged in groups based on similarities in their appearance or shape and form; additional common similar species are noted where needed. Thus, examining the structural details of your specimen and comparing it with the accompanying text and color photographs form the primary basis for identification.

With your specimen mushroom in hand, identification can sometimes be accomplished by thumbing through the illustrations until a match is found. Although this procedure sometimes works, having to look at and compare all of the illustrations with the unknown fungus is relatively inefficient. A more efficient approach is to use the illustrations in combination with the identification outline to major groups of fungi, printed at the end of the book. The outline can quickly lead the user to the appropriate group of photographs.

You will find it helpful to briefly study and make notes on the visible features of the unidentified mushroom before using the outline. Make reference to the checklist of field characters printed at the end of the Introduction. This procedure will sharpen your observational powers and result in greater accuracy and confidence in the identification.

In all cases, if you believe your specimen matches one of the illustrations, carefully compare it with both the photograph and the written data on the facing page. Because not all mushrooms are illustrated in this (or any other) book, be sure to read the information under "Similar Species" in each description. If your specimen does not fully agree with the description, either you have made an error and should try again or your specimen is a species not included in this book.

Notes on Plate Descriptions

Each photograph included in this guide shows characteristic features that will assist in recognition and identification of specimens collected. Each one is accompanied by a description of key features required for proper identification. In addition, a brief discussion of similar species is provided. No guide contains all known mushrooms, but many common ones likely to be encountered are included in this book.

Measurements of mushrooms described in this guide, such as cap diameter and stalk length and thickness, are given in metric units. Although English units are more familiar to many people, the metric system is used in science and most scientific books and reference works. The more serious enthusiast who consults monographs or technical papers will discover that all measurements are given in the metric system. The most commonly used measurements for describing mushroom characteristics are compared with the English inch below:

1 inch = 2½ centimeters (approximately)
1 centimeter (cm) = ⅖ inch (approximately) = 10 mm
1 millimeter (mm) = ⅒ cm = 1000 μm
1 micrometer (μm) = ⅟₁₀₀₀ mm

For field use and visual comparison of metric units and their English equivalents, rulers with both kinds of units has been reproduced inside the cover of this guide. With a little practice, metric measures become easy to use.

Spores and other microscopic features are much too small to be measured accurately with an ordinary ruler. Instead, they are measured with a very small, precision glass ruler calibrated in micrometers (microns). This device, called an ocular micrometer, is inserted into one eyepiece of a microscope and allows accurate measurement of microscopic dimensions. Further information on microscopic features is given in the back of the book.

Common Name: A common name is provided whenever one has been previously reported. Where two names are widely used, both are listed. Many common names represent attempts to translate Latin scientific names; in many instances these translations are not totally accurate. Many mushrooms do not have a common name at all. No new common names have been introduced in this guide.

Scientific Name: The Latin scientific name is provided for each species. The science of mushroom classification is still in a state of flux, and a scientific name may be changed if a species is reclassified. If the name used has resulted from a recent reclassification, the former name is noted in the comments section.

As do species of all other living things, each mushroom species has its own unique scientific name. It consists of two parts and is often descriptive of the color, shape, or size of the mushroom, the place where it is found, or the person who first collected it. The first part is the genus name; its first letter is always capitalized. The second part is the species designator (epithet); all its letters are lower case. For example, in the species name *Lactarius rufus*, *Lactarius* describes a genus comprising several species of mushrooms—the milk mushrooms. The species epithet *rufus* means "red" and refers to the cap color of this species.

The use of scientific names is highly recommended. Many mushrooms have no common name, others have more than one, and the same common name may be used for different mushroom species in different parts of the continent. Scientific names are not as difficult as they may appear; with a little practice and experience, they quickly become familiar.

Edibility: If known to be so, the species is listed as "edible." Although somewhat subjective, the word "choice" is added to indicate those mushrooms which, in our opinion, have exceptional flavor and texture. Some species are listed as "inedible" because of a tough texture or unpleasant taste or both. Symptoms caused by species listed as poisonous are often described in the comments section. Many species are categorized as "edibility unknown" because no information is available about them—**they should not be eaten.** Be certain to read the section *Guidelines for Eating Wild Mushrooms*. Important references on the subject of mushroom poisoning are listed under "Further Reading" in the back of the book.

Visible Features: For true mushrooms, the features described include cap, gills, and stalk. Descriptions of mushrooms with a different shape—cup fungi, club fungi, puffballs, bird's nest fungi, and coral fungi—include color, shape, size, and any other readily observable features that aid in identification. Flesh color, texture, thickness, odor, and color change caused by injury are also noted for most species. Cap descriptions include size, shape, color, texture, and other features such as marginal grooves or central knob when present. Gills, pores, or spines are mentioned whenever present; gill descriptions include notes on attachment, spacing, color, production of latex when cut, and color change when injured. The presence or absence of a stalk is recorded, and if it is present, the description includes length, thickness, shape, surface texture, color, and color change when injured. Additional features such as a ring, cup, veil, or warts are described when present.

Spore Color/Print: Spore color is a valuable, reliable, and easily obtained and determined characteristic for mushroom identification. For most species spore color is best determined by making a spore print, as described elsewhere in this introduction. For puffballs and other species that do not produce spore prints, the color of the spores can usually be seen inside or on the surface of the mature fruiting body.

Fruiting: The pattern in which the mushroom grows (solitary, scattered, in loose groups, or in loose or tight clusters), the habitat where it is found, and the seasons(s) when it fruits are listed. The fruiting season assumes typical weather conditions; mushrooms may occur outside the seasons stated whenever weather conditions are unusual. For example, an early spring with temperatures above normal may cause some summer mushrooms to appear ahead of their normal fruiting period.

Range: The general known North American distribution of species is provided. The range of some mushrooms is well established, but the distribution of many other species is poorly known. Therefore, it may be possible to find a species outside of its stated range.

Family: The family name for each described species is included for purposes of classification. (Family is the next largest category after genus in biological classification.) Mushrooms that belong to the same family have similar features, and many of these are evident as field characters. Species in the inky cap family, *Coprinaceae*, for example, all have very dark spore prints— usually dark brown, purple-black, or black.

Comments: Included here are warnings and cautions, brief notes on symptoms of mushroom poisoning (where appropriate), the reason(s) for an inedible species being so, former scientific names, unusual features, and other significant information.

Similar Species: Although some mushrooms have such distinctive characteristics that they are not likely to be confused with other species, most are similar or nearly identical in appearance to one or more others. The reliability of your identification depends on your comparing your find with both the illustrated (primary) species and those noted in the text under "Similar Species." If your specimen does not fully agree with the description, either you have made an error or your specimen is a species not included in this book.

Although this guide emphasizes visible features, information about the microscopic features of spores of all species described (including those noted under "Similar Species") is presented in table form in the section following the species descriptions and plates. Spore size, shape, color, surface features, and Melzer's reagent (amyloid) reaction are included.

How to Make a Spore Print

The process of precise mushroom identification always includes the making of a spore print whenever possible. Even though individual spores cannot be seen without a microscope, a spore print, which results from the deposit of a very large number of spores in a small area, will reveal spore color. It is a valuable supportive characteristic for the identification of many mushroom species.

To make a spore print, use only fresh, unrefrigerated, mature caps. Cut off the stalk of the mushroom and place the cap gill-side, pore-side, or spine-side down on a piece of white paper or pieces of black paper and white paper positioned side by side. We routinely use $2'' \times 4''$ paper strips, which can serve alternatively as field labels and for short field notes. It may be useful to make a part of the spore print on a glass slide or a glass or plastic coverslip. To do this, place the slide or coverslip under the mushroom cap and on top of the paper on which you make your normal spore print. In that way, you can get a spore deposit on both the paper and the glass at the same time. Cover the cap and paper with a container such as a drinking glass, cup, or bowl or wrap them in waxed paper to prevent air movement. Examine the paper after a few hours. A spore print may be visible in 1 to 15 hours, depending upon the species and the age of the mushroom.

For determination of spore print color, heavy deposits are always best, but thin prints are more helpful than none at all. Spore print colors should *always* be determined from a print made on white paper because pale-tinted spores (cream, pale yellow, pale pink, and the like) will appear white if observed only on black paper. If the spore print is light in color and thin, it may not be easily observable on the white paper, but its presence will be obvious on the black paper and/or coverslip. The color of a spore print on glass can be determined by holding the glass over white paper. Spores collected on glass or plastic can also be used in the Melzer's reagent test, outlined in the back of the book. Compare your spore print results with the information provided in the descriptions. It is also helpful to record the results for future reference.

A spore print can be initiated in the field by preparing the specimen as described above, wrapping it in waxed paper, and placing it flat in the bottom of the collecting basket. Often, such specimens will have produced usable spore prints by the time you arrive home.

Spore prints cannot be obtained from some mushrooms, such as puffballs, bird's nest fungi, and stinkhorns. In some of these cases the spore color can be determined by looking at the internal or surface spore mass. In other cases, identification must be based entirely on other characteristics.

Collecting Mushrooms

A field trip to collect mushrooms requires careful attention to the ground, logs, stumps, branches, leaves, moss, and standing trees. Many mushrooms are easily overlooked because they blend in with vegetation or are often partially covered by leaves or humus on the forest floor. In areas with dense ground cover, some mushroom hunters use a cane or stick to brush plants aside and uncover mushrooms that otherwise may go undetected.

Mushrooms should be carefully removed from the substrates on which they grow; be certain to include any structures partially buried in the soil or wood. Careless picking may leave behind important structures needed for identification. Specimens should be wrapped in waxed paper, *not* in plastic bags, and carefully placed in the collecting basket. Wrapping keeps collections separate and helps prevent the mixing of edible and poisonous species. Furthermore, waxed paper prolongs freshness, whereas plastic bags, because of their moisture-trapping capacity and lack of air exchange, cause mushrooms to deteriorate rapidly. A general wrapping procedure is to put a row of mushrooms of the same species on a sheet of waxed paper, roll the paper into a tube with the mushrooms inside (going several times around the specimens, if possible), and twist the ends several times to close the package.

Mushrooms collected for eating should be fresh and free of insect larvae. To check for larvae, cut off the base of the stalk and examine it for pencil-lead-size worm tunnels. When in doubt, cut the mushroom lengthwise into two pieces. The presence of small white to yellowish brown larvae and/or their tunnels is evidence of infestation, and the mushroom should be discarded.

When gathering mushrooms for identification, collect specimens in as many stages of development as possible. Identification of some species requires examination of the very young "button" stages as well as more mature ones. Try to wrap all the stages for each species in a single package. Two or more packages may be needed for large collections. Tiny, fragile specimens may be enclosed by moss or other surrounding substrates in which they grow and placed in small tin containers or plastic boxes for added protection.

It is important to record a few notes for each collection and include the notes with the mushrooms in the waxed paper package. The information should include the substrate on which the mushrooms were growing, the types of surrounding trees, if known, and the pattern in which the mushrooms were growing—single, scattered about, in loose groups, or clustered together.

Do not leave mushrooms in bags or baskets sitting in the sun or back of a car on hot days. They will rapidly deteriorate and begin to decompose. An ice chest or cooler will help in transporting collections in vehicles during the warmer months.

Since many characteristics, such as color, odor, and moisture level, change after picking, mushrooms should be identified as soon after collecting as possible. Members of the genus *Corpinus,* commonly called Inky Caps, form enzymes that change their tissues into a black inky fluid even in the refrigerator; therefore, they should be identified and cooked (if edible) on the day of collection. Cooking stops the enzymatic breakdown, and the mushrooms can then be stored in the refrigerator for a few days. Most other mushrooms may be refrigerated in their packages overnight until you are ready to identify them. Unfortunately, refrigeration often suppresses distinctive odors that can be helpful in identification.

Guidelines for Eating Wild Mushrooms

Wild mushrooms have a sinister reputation that is widespread and often undeserved. Although fatalities are reported each year from ingestion of deadly species, the vast majority of reported poisonings consist of gastrointestinal symptoms such as nausea, vomiting, cramps, and diarrhea. One should not, however, throw caution to the wind and take chances with unknown species. Learning how to study and identify species, and thus distinguish edible from poisonous ones, will enable the mushroom hunter to safely select mushrooms for the table.

At present, fewer than a dozen North American mushroom species are known to have caused fatalities; about 200 other species are considered poisonous. Several hundred species are considered nonpoisonous—either edible or inedible (because of unpleasant taste, tough texture, or small size). The edibility of the several thousand remaining species is unknown. As in times past, many people refer to edible species as mushrooms and poisonous ones as toadstools and claim to be able to distinguish them easily by some rule of thumb. In truth, no such simple differentiation can be made. The edibility or toxicity of a mushroom is a chemical attribute unrelated to visible features. Edible and poisonous species are differentiated only by knowing the species—by recognizing and identifying species according to field characters and microscopic features—and by knowing which species are edible and which are not. Rules of thumb concerning poisonous mushrooms can be dangerous. Avoid them. For example, although it is true that some poisonous mushrooms will tarnish a silver coin, so will some edible species (and cauliflower, too!), while some poisonous ones will not. To be certain, learn how to identify the species and follow these guidelines:

1. **Eat only those species you are able to identify with certainty.** "When in doubt, throw it out," or obtain professional assistance for confirmation. Do not learn about edibility through uneducated experimentation.

2. Unless this guide states otherwise, wild mushrooms should be thoroughly cooked and not eaten raw. Many species contain toxic substances that are dissipated by thorough heating.

3. Eat only specimens that are fresh and free of insect larvae. Spoiled or infected mushrooms may result in gastric upset and cause you to incriminate the mushroom rather than the bacteria or larvae within.

4. Some mushroom species can be eaten safely by most people but may cause adverse reactions in some individuals. When eating a species for the first time, consume only a small portion. Gradually increase the amount each time you find it again until you are certain that it has no adverse effects.

5. Avoid overeating. Some mushrooms are safe when consumed in moderation but poisonous when eaten in large amounts.

6. Do not let wild or domestic animals be your guide to edibility. Differences in animal physiology may allow them to safely consume mushrooms that are poisonous to humans.

7. Save one or two intact and uncooked mushrooms in the refrigerator for at least 48 hours after eating a species new to you. These can be used as reference specimens in case symptoms of poisoning develop.

8. If mushroom poisoning is suspected, consult your physician and your regional Poison Control Information Center. Telephone numbers for the nearest regional Poison Control Information Center are listed among the emergency numbers in the front of many telephone directories.

For information on mushroom poisoning, consult the references listed under "Further Reading" in the back of the book.

Collecting and eating wild mushrooms can be a safe and enjoyable experience, but carelessness and the taking of chances can be fatal!

Checklist of Field Characters

See also the illustrated glossary in the front of the book.

I. How and Where Specimens Grow
    A. How: sometimes characteristic of particular species
        1. Solitary: only one present
        2. Scattered: several growing singly in the same general area
        3. In groups (gregarious): grouped rather close together
        4. In clusters (caespitose): adhering to one another
        (In 2, 3, and 4, individual mushrooms arise from the same mycelium.)
    B. Where: materials on which specimens grow (substrate)
        1. On the ground, in earth (terrestrial)
        2. On dung (coprophilous)
        3. On wood (lignicolous)
        4. On leaves (epiphyllous)
    C. Plant associates: Note nearby trees, shrubs, and/or other plants. Some mushrooms form associations with plant roots (mycorrhizal associations); others may have restricted nutrient requirements, i.e., may require specific kinds of leaves or other matter on which to grow. In forested habitats, if associate species are not known, the general category of trees present (conifers, hardwoods, mixed) may be useful to note.

II. Cap (pileus) Shape and Structure
    A. Diameter: varies (within limits) with age, moisture conditions, etc.
    B. Shape (varies with age): convex, bell-shaped (campanulate), conical, with a central knob (umbonate), flat (plane), depressed, uplifted, or funnel-shaped (infundibuliform)
    C. Edge (margin)
        1. In side view: inrolled, incurved, decurved, or flat (plane)
        2. In top view: entire, eroded, rimose, or appendiculate (due to veil)
    D. Striations (lines or grooves): may be evident at the cap edge
        1. Gills visible as translucent lines seen through the cap edge (translucent-striate)
        2. Lines part of the cap itself (striate)
        3. Striations formed by shallow grooves (sulcate)
        4. Bumps present on the surface of the striations (tuberculate-striate)
        5. Striations formed by folds and grooves, somewhat like an expanded accordion or fan (plicate-striate)
    E. Surface: conditions often vary with age, maturity, weather, etc. Examine numerous specimens and note weather conditions at the time.
        1. Moisture condition
            a) Dry: usually dull in appearance
           b) Moist. Note that a mushroom's color sometimes fades sharply and quickly upon slight drying; such species are called hygrophanous.
           c) Sticky or slimy to the touch (viscid); usually shiny when dry. If a specimen is dry but suspected of being viscid, test by moistening a fingertip and rubbing the cap.
           d) Extremely viscid, with a thick, often oozing slime (glutinous)

2. Texture. Texture conditions are usually associated with dry to moist surfaces, but some terms here may be used to describe species with viscid surfaces as well.
   a) Covered with interwoven fine fibrils (fibrillose)
   b) Having scales on the surface (scaly)
   c) Fibrils arranged in groups or bundles to form scales (fibrillose-scaly)
   d) Scales upright, at least at their tips, about the center of the cap (squarrose)
   e) Smooth, without fibrils, scales, or other decorations (glabrous)
   f) Velvety (tomentose or velutinous)
   g) Powdery (pruinose)
3. Color
   a) Variations between young, mature, and old specimens (check all if available)
   b) Variations due to moisture level (note color in the field at time of collection)
   c) Changes that occur on bruising
   d) Changes that occur after picking (in hygrophanous species)
4. Universal veil remnants (if present). Note abundance and distribution, form, consistency, and color.
F. Flesh (context)
   1. Thickness: at the center and at the edge
   2. Texture: soft, hard, fragile, tough, etc.
   3. Color: both normal appearance and any changes that occur on bruising or exposure to air
   4. Odor: bleach-like, anise-like, almond extract-like, garlic-like, etc.
   5. Taste: mild, bitter, acrid or peppery, mealy-metallic (farinaceous), disagreeable, etc. **Caution: DO NOT SWALLOW. Spit out thoroughly after tasting. Your specimen could be poisonous.**
   6. Latex
      a) Present or absent
      b) If present, note color and color change (if any) on exposure to air, and taste.

III. Gills (lamellae)
   A. Attachment to or association with the stalk (stipe): varies with age, so check young, mature, and old specimens.
      1. Attached: descending the stalk (decurrent), subdecurrent, emarginate, adnate, notched (sinuate), adnexed, or seceding
      2. Free of the stalk
   B. Spacing (terms below are relative, judged in relation to cap size)
      1. Crowded together (crowded): gills so close together that spaces between them are not easily distinguished
      2. Closely spaced (close): gills close together, but spaces between them are distinct
      3. Somewhat separated (subdistant): intermediate between closely spaced and widely spaced
      4. Widely spaced (distant): gills set far apart, especially at cap edge
   C. Color
      1. Variations between young, mature, and old specimens
      2. Changes that occur on bruising
      3. Color of latex, if present; changes that occur on exposure to air; and whether latex causes any changes in the color of gill tissues

D. Thickness (width or distance between the flat faces of a gill; usually relative to cap size)
   1. Thin
   2. Thick
E. Depth (distance from the cap to the gill edge; usually relative to cap size)
   1. Narrow
   2. Moderately broad
   3. Broad
F. Margin
   1. Smooth
   2. Fringed (fimbriate); often most easily seen with a hand lens
   3. Toothed or jagged like a saw's edge (serrate)
   4. Edges colored differently from the faces (marginate)
G. Lamellulae: small gills that do not extend to the stalk; described by numbers of series, or tiers, between pairs of full gills

IV. Stalk (stipe)
   A. Size: somewhat variable; determine ranges
      1. Length (base to apex)
      2. Width (at the apex)
   B. Shape (may vary with age)
   C. Surface
      1. Moisture condition
         a) Dry
         b) Moist
         c) Viscid (check for presence or absence of a viscid veil)
      2. Texture
         a) Covered with soft, downy hairs (pubescent); often best seen with a hand lens
         b) Other surface variations as those listed under "Cap"
            Note: scales on the stalk surfaces are often veil remnants. Examine young specimens to determine origin of scales, if present.
      3. Color
         a) Variations between young, mature, and old specimens
         b) Changes that occur on bruising, if any
         c) Color and color changes of latex, if present
   D. Flesh
      1. Texture
         a) Solid and uniform (solid)
         b) Not homogeneous, with a central "core" (stuffed)
         c) Central core empty (hollow)
      2. Color and color changes on exposure to air
   E. Presence or absence of a ring (annulus), constituting the remnant of a partial veil
      1. General position: apical, basal, or central
      2. Persistent or disappearing (fugacious); if persistent, may be attached or movable
      3. Structure
         a) Membranous: more or less sheet-like and flaring, or (if thin) collapsed against the stalk; may be single or double (look for undersurface patches that indicate double)
         b) Pad-like, bracelet-like, or cottony (this type does not flare out)
         c) Cobwebby
      4. Color

F. Presence or absence of a cup (volva) at the base, constituting the remnant of a universal veil
1. Shape
2. Texture
   a) Membranous: a free, well-formed cup (on the cap, veil remnants may be lacking, or one to a few large patches may be left)
   b) Fragile: usually in the form of zones (wart-like, band-like, or bracelet-like) intergrown with the stalk surface at the base (often leaving many warts as remnants on the cap surface)
G. Other characteristics sometimes present
1. Profuse mycelium at the base
2. Colored mycelium at the base
3. Rope-like strands (rhizomorphs) running from the mushroom to the substrate
V. Spore Color (Note: Gill color is not always the same as spore color.)
A. Spore print on white paper
B. Spore deposits from other, overhanging caps
C. Spore mass on surface or interior (for puffballs, stinkhorns, and other species that do not form spore prints)

Sequence of Plates

BIRD'S NEST FUNGI

White-egg Bird's Nest, *Crucibulum laeve*   INEDIBLE

Fruiting Body: 5–10 mm tall, 5–10 mm wide at the top; cup-shaped to cone-shaped. Outer surface hairy, yellow-brown to dark brown; inner surface smooth, yellowish brown; covered by a hairy, yellowish orange lid in young specimens. Contains several thin, white to pale yellow, 1–2 mm wide, disc-shaped "eggs," each with a very small, pouch-like purse on the underside. **Stalk:** Absent. **Spore Color:** White. **Fruiting:** Solitary or more commonly scattered to clustered on wood chips, twigs, and branches; summer, fall. **Range:** Throughout N. America. **Family:** Nidulariaceae. **Comments:** Known as *C. vulgare* in older references. The tiny "eggs" with spores inside are spread over distances of several feet by the splash of raindrops or dripping water falling into the cups. **Similar Species:** All other species of bird's nest fungi have dark-colored "eggs."

Nidula niveo-tomentosa   INEDIBLE

Fruiting Body: 4–6 mm tall; mug-like (sides parallel), flaring, up to 5 mm wide at the apex. Outer surface finely hairy, white, becoming yellow to gray when old; inner surface smooth, white near the apex, tan below; young specimens covered by a granular, cinnamon lid. Contains numerous dark brown, disc-like "eggs," 0.5–1 mm across, immersed in a clear gelatin-like material. **Stalk:** Absent. **Spore Color:** White. **Fruiting:** Scattered or in groups on decaying woody debris (twigs, woody vines, and fern leaf bases) and forest floor litter; fall, winter; also spring (after snow melting) and summer (after thunderstorms) at high elevations. **Range:** Pacific Northwest—British Columbia to Calif. **Family:** Nidulariaceae. **Comments:** Also known as *N. microcarpa*. The "eggs" of *Nidula* species lack the small, pouch-like purse on their central undersurface. **Similar Species:** Common Gel Bird's Nest (*Nidula candida*; inedible) has larger (1.5–3 mm wide), light brown "eggs" and larger, more funnel-shaped cups with a coarser, more scruffy, cinnamon to gray outer surface. Pea-shaped Nidularia (*Nidularia pulvinata*; inedible) forms its "eggs" within a cinnamon, cushion-shaped (rather than cup-shaped) fruiting body.

Cyathus stercoreus   INEDIBLE

Fruiting Body: 5–15 mm tall, 4–8 mm wide at the top; cone-shaped to cup-shaped. Outer surface coarsely hairy, yellow-brown to red-brown (or nearly black in older specimens); inner surface smooth, lead gray or bluish black; covered by a hairy, yellow-brown to red-brown lid in young specimens. Contains several thin, bluish black, disc-shaped "eggs," 0.5–2 mm wide, each with a small, pouch-like purse on the underside. **Stalk:** Absent. **Spore Color:** White. **Fruiting:** Scattered to clustered on wood chips, old dung piles, and well-manured soil; summer, fall. **Range:** Throughout N. America. **Family:** Nidulariaceae. **Comments:** This species is highly variable in shape and color, resulting in a long list of synonymous names. **Similar Species:** Black Egg Bird's Nest (*C. olla*; inedible) has a smooth, gray or gray-brown fruiting body with widely flaring upper edges and large (up to 3.5 mm wide), irregularly shaped "eggs"; it is found on soil, wood, and plant debris. Splash Cups (*C. striatus*; inedible) have reddish brown to chocolate brown to gray-brown fruiting bodies with distinct lines or grooves on the shiny inner surface; the "eggs" are grayish to gray-brown.

▲ White-egg Bird's Nest, *Crucibulum laeve*

▲ *Nidula niveo-tomentosa*

▼ *Cyathus stercoreus*

CUP AND DISC FUNGI

Orange Peel, *Aleuria aurantia*   EDIBLE

Fruiting Body: 2.5–10 cm wide; cup-shaped to disc-shaped or saucer-like. Inner (upper) surface smooth, bright orange to yellow-orange; outer (lower) surface smooth, pale yellowish orange. Flesh thin, bright orange to yellow-orange. **Spore Color:** White. **Fruiting:** Solitary, scattered, or in large clusters on the ground on lawns, in gardens, along roadsides, and on disturbed soil; late spring, summer, fall. **Range:** Widespread throughout N. America. **Family:** Pyronemataceae. **Comments:** This mushroom is quite brittle and is easily broken when handled. **Similar Species:** Blue-staining Cup (*Caloscypha fulgens*; edibility unknown) is also yellow-orange but develops dark olive green to blue-green stains, especially on the outer (lower) surface.

Yellow Fairy Cups, *Bisporella citrina*   EDIBILITY UNKNOWN

Fruiting Body: 1–3 mm wide; disc-shaped to shallowly cup-shaped. Inner (upper) surface smooth, bright yellow; outer (lower) surface pale yellow. Flesh thin, bright yellow. **Stalk:** Broad, short to nearly absent; pale yellow. **Spore Color:** White. **Fruiting:** In large clusters on decaying wood, especially hardwood; spring, summer, fall. **Range:** Throughout N. America. **Family:** Leotiaceae. **Comments:** Fruiting bodies of this species may be so numerous that their shapes are distorted by overcrowding. **Similar Species:** Acorn Cup (*Hymenoscyphus fructigenus*; edibility unknown) can be found on fallen acorns and hickory nuts. Green Stain Fungus (*Chlorociboria aeruginascens*; edibility unknown) forms blue-green cups and stains wood bluish green.

Hairy Rubber Cup, *Galiella rufa*   EDIBILITY UNKNOWN

Fruiting Body: 1–3 cm wide; cup-shaped. Inner (upper) surface smooth, reddish brown to tan; outer (lower) surface covered with minute hairs, dark brown to brownish black. Flesh thick, watery to gel-like to rubbery. **Stalk:** Up to 1 cm long, 3–5 mm thick; with dense, minute, dark brown to black hairs; absent in some specimens. **Spore Color:** White. **Fruiting:** Solitary to clustered on rotting hardwood; spring, summer, fall. **Range:** Eastern N. America, west to Minn., Iowa, and Mo. **Family:** Sarcosomataceae. **Comments:** Very young stages may look like a puffball, but the cup-like shape develops with age. **Similar Species:** Hairy Black Cup (*Pseudoplectania nigrella*; edibility unknown) is a stalkless, black cup with a hairy outer (lower) surface. Brown-haired White Cup (*Humaria hemisphaerica*; edibility unknown) is a stalkless cup with a white to grayish white inner (upper) surface and hairy, brown outer (lower) surface. Neither has thick, gelatinous flesh.

▲ Orange Peel
Aleuria aurantia

▲ Yellow Fairy Cups
Bisporella citrina

Hairy Rubber Cup ▶
Galiella rufa

CUP AND DISC FUNGI

Scarlet Cup, *Sarcoscypha coccinea* EDIBILITY UNKNOWN
Fruiting Body: 2–7 cm wide; disc-shaped to deeply cup-shaped. Inner (upper) surface bright red with incurved edges; outer (lower) surface somewhat fuzzy, white to yellowish white. Flesh brittle, whitish. **Stalk:** Typically 1–2 cm long, 3–5 mm thick; white; often absent. **Spore Color:** White. **Fruiting:** Solitary or in small clusters on decaying hardwood branches partially covered by leaves; spring (also winter on the West Coast). **Range:** Eastern N. America and West Coast. **Family:** Sarcoscyphaceae. **Comments:** This is one of the earliest mushrooms to appear in spring, often (in the East) beneath melting snow. **Similar Species:** Stalked Scarlet Cup (*S. occidentalis*; edibility unknown) is smaller and has a longer stalk; it is found throughout the eastern U.S., west to Kan. and Neb.

Eyelash Cup, *Scutellinia scutellata* EDIBILITY UNKNOWN
Fruiting Body: 5–20 mm wide; shallowly cup-shaped, aging to flat. Inner (upper) surface smooth, reddish orange; outer (lower) surface pale orange, covered with numerous stiff brown hairs projecting from the cup edge. Flesh thin, brittle, pale orange to reddish orange. **Stalk:** Absent. **Spore Color:** White. **Fruiting:** In dense clusters on decaying wood and damp soil; late spring, summer, fall. **Range:** Throughout N. America. **Family:** Pyronemataceae. **Comments:** Many other species of *Scutellinia* grow on wood and soil; nearly identical in appearance, they require microscopic examination for identification. **Similar Species:** Burn Site Ochre Cup (*Anthracobia melaloma*; edibility unknown) has a yellow-brown inner (upper) surface and short dark hairs on the outer (lower) surface; it grows on burned soil and charred wood. *Cheilymenia* species are yellower and have pale yellow or light brown hairs. Many other species have a similar appearance and are difficult to identify by field characters alone.

Moose Antlers, *Wynnea americana* EDIBILITY UNKNOWN
Fruiting Body: 2–10 cm wide, 5–12 cm high; consisting of several elongated, ear-shaped or antler-shaped branches. Outer surface dark brown to nearly black; inner surface pinkish orange to reddish orange to pale reddish brown. Flesh thick, firm. **Stalk:** 1–2 cm long, 5–10 mm thick; arising underground from a fibrous, brown, irregular to rounded mass of tissue. **Spore Color:** White. **Fruiting:** Solitary or in groups on the ground in hardwood forests (never abundant); summer, fall. **Range:** Widely distributed in eastern N. America. **Family:** Sarcoscyphaceae. **Comments:** The cluster of vertically elongated, ear-like branches that are brown on the outer surface and pinkish orange to pale reddish brown on the inner surface is characteristic. **Similar Species:** Stalked Cauliflower Fungus (*W. sparassoides*; edibility unknown) has a yellow-brown cauliflower-like head on a long brown stalk.

▲ Scarlet Cup
Sarcoscypha coccinea

Eyelash Cup ▶
Scutellinia scutellata

▼ Moose Antlers
Wynnea americana

STINKHORNS

Netted Stinkhorn, *Dictyophora duplicata*   INEDIBLE

Fruiting Body: 12–15 cm tall overall; head 3–5 cm tall, 3–4 cm wide, pitted, with a white-rimmed opening at the apex and covered with a slimy, foul-smelling, greenish brown spore mass. Flesh thin, soft, white. **Stalk:** 8–12 cm tall, 2–4 cm thick; spongy; white; interior hollow; surrounded at the apex by a white, net-like veil that emerges from below the head. The stalk arises from a thick, oval, internally gelatinous, white (bruising pink to pinkish lilac), egg-shaped mass that is anchored to the ground by one or more thick, dull white (bruising pink to pinkish lilac) cords. **Spore Color:** White. **Fruiting:** Solitary, scattered, or in groups on the ground in hardwood forests; summer, fall. **Range:** Eastern N. America, Canada to Fla., west to Iowa. **Family:** Phallaceae. **Comments:** The foul-smelling spore masses of stinkhorns attract insects, which distribute the spores; one often smells these mushrooms before seeing them. **Similar Species:** Common Stinkhorn (*Phallus impudicus,* inedible) has a similarly pitted head, and Ravenel's Stinkhorn (*P. ravenelii;* inedible) has a smooth head; both, however, lack the white, net-like veil.

Ravenel's Stinkhorn, *Phallus ravenelii*   INEDIBLE

Fruiting Body: 10–16 cm tall overall; head 3–4.5 cm long, 1.5–4 cm wide, with a dishrag-like surface and a white-rimmed opening at the apex; head covered with a slimy, foul-smelling, greenish brown to olive brown spore mass. Flesh thin, white. **Stalk:** 10–16 cm long, 1.5–3 cm thick; arising from a thick, oval, internally gelatinous, white, egg-shaped mass that is anchored to the ground by one or more thick white cords (often branched); sponge-like, fragile, white to cream. **Spore Color:** White. **Fruiting:** Solitary to scattered or clustered, on or around well-decayed logs, in woody debris, and in wood chips (in gardens); summer, fall. **Range:** Eastern N. America. **Family:** Phallaceae. **Comments:** Stinkhorns in the unexpanded ("egg") stage are reportedly edible. **Similar Species:** Common Stinkhorn (*P. impudicus;* inedible) and Netted Stinkhorn (*Dictyophora duplicata;* inedible) are similar in general form but have a pitted (rather than dishrag-like) head surface.

Dog Stinkhorn, *Mutinus caninus*   INEDIBLE

Fruiting Body: 6–10 cm long, 8–11 mm thick; head absent; sponge-like; pinkish red to pale pink; upper quarter covered with a foul-smelling, slimy, greenish brown spore mass. **Stalk:** Arising from an ovoid to ellipsoid, internally gelatinous, white, egg-shaped mass that is anchored to the ground by one or more thick white cords; fragile; interior hollow. **Spore Color:** White. **Fruiting:** Solitary to scattered in soil and humus (in hardwood forests) and mulch and wood chips (in gardens); summer, fall. **Range:** Widespread in eastern N. America. **Family:** Phallaceae. **Comments:** A white variety of this species, *M. caninus* var. *albus* (inedible; *see photo*), is sometimes encountered in the Pacific Northwest and northern Midwest (U.S.). **Similar Species:** Elegant Stinkhorn (*M. elegans;* inedible) has the slimy spore mass over the upper third of a tapered, pinkish to pale orange stalk.

Netted Stinkhorn ▶
Dictyophora duplicata

▼ Ravenel's Stinkhorn
Phallus ravenelii

▼ Dog Stinkhorn
Mutinus caninus

▼ *Mutinus caninus* var. *albus*

CORAL AND SIMILAR FUNGI

White Worm Coral, *Clavaria vermicularis*   EDIBLE

Fruiting Body: 3–12 cm tall, 2–5 mm thick; upright, tapering, spindle-shaped to worm-like cylinders, frequently fused into clusters; white, sometimes yellowish at the tips. Flesh brittle, white. **Stalk:** Absent except as the fused base of the fruiting bodies. **Spore Print:** White. **Fruiting:** In small to large clusters on the ground in woods and fields; summer, fall. **Range:** Widely distributed throughout N. America. **Family:** Clavariaceae. **Comments:** The fruiting bodies often become flattened and curved with age. **Similar Species:** Yellow Coral (*Clavulinopsis fusiformis;* edible) is bright yellow, spindle-shaped, and occasionally branched; Purple Club Coral (*Clavaria purpurea;* edible) is grayish purple. Both grow in clusters on the ground. White Coral (*Ramariopsis kunzii;* edible) has white to pinkish white branches with short, prong-like tips; it grows on the ground. *Clavaria zollingeri* (edibility unknown) has deep violet branches and a disagreeable taste. *Clavaria rubicundula* (edibility unknown) forms tall, unbranched, pinkish gray to pinkish brown stalks; it fruits in dense clusters on the ground.

Carbon Antlers, *Xylaria hypoxylon*   INEDIBLE

Fruiting Body: 3–8 cm tall, 2–8 mm wide; cylindrical to flattened, sometimes twisted, often branched, with round to tapered tips. Upper part at first white and powdery (from asexual spores), aging to gray to gray-black, becoming minutely roughened from the protruding tips of small, embedded, spore-containing flasks. Flesh very tough, white. **Spore Color:** Dark brown to black. **Fruiting:** Scattered to clustered on fallen tree branches in forests; summer and fall in the East, fall (north) to winter (south) along the West Coast. **Range:** Throughout N. America. **Family:** Xylariaceae. **Comments:** Also known as Candle Snuff Fungus. Its small size and tough texture make this species useless for the table. **Similar Species:** Dead Man's Fingers (*X. polymorpha;* edibility unknown) is much thicker and occurs scattered or in clusters on dead branches and buried wood of hardwoods, especially beech, in eastern N. America.

Orange-colored Cordyceps, *Cordyceps militaris*   INEDIBLE

Head: 1–4 cm tall, 2–6 mm wide; cylindrical, sometimes longitudinally furrowed, rounded to tapered at the apex. Surface minutely roughened from the protruding tips of small, embedded, spore-containing flasks; orange to reddish orange. Flesh orange. **Stalk:** 1–5 cm long, 3–5 mm thick; smooth; orange to reddish orange (like the head). **Spore Color:** White. **Fruiting:** Solitary or in groups on buried larvae and pupae of moths and butterflies; summer, fall. **Range:** Throughout N. America where the hosts occur. **Family:** Clavicipitaceae. **Comments:** Easily broken off of the buried larvae or pupae; specimens must be carefully dug up. **Similar Species:** Rhinoceros Beetle Cordyceps (*C. melolonthae;* edibility unknown; *see photo*) is larger, pale to bright yellow, and grows on buried beetle larvae; it occurs in eastern N. America.

▲ White Worm Coral
Clavaria vermicularis

◄ Carbon Antlers
Xylaria hypoxylon

right:
Orange-colored Cordyceps ▶
Cordyceps militaris

far right:
Rhinoceros Beetle Cordyceps ▶
Cordyceps melolonthae

CORAL AND SIMILAR FUNGI

Flat-topped Coral, *Clavariadelphus truncatus*   EDIBLE

Fruiting Body: 6–15 cm tall, 2–7 cm thick at the top, tapering downward to 1–3 cm at the base; club-shaped, flattened and often wrinkled at the top; yellow-orange to pinkish brown. Flesh spongy, thick, white; taste sweet in fresh specimens. **Stalk:** Indistinct; base covered with white hairs. **Spore Print:** Pale yellow-brown. **Fruiting:** Solitary, scattered, or in groups on the ground in conifer woods; summer, fall. **Range:** Throughout N. America. **Family:** Clavariaceae. **Comments:** Older specimens may split open, revealing a hollow interior. **Similar Species:** Pestle-shaped Coral (*C. pistillaris*; edible) has a rounded top, a bitter taste, and is found under hardwoods. *C. ligula* (edibility unknown) is much smaller and has a cylindrical shape; it is salmon-colored and has a bitter taste.

Light Red Coral, *Ramaria araiospora*   EDIBLE (caution)

Fruiting Body: 5–12 cm tall, 2–8 cm wide; upright and highly branched; pinkish orange to pale red branches with small, pink to yellow-orange tips. Flesh thick, firm, white. **Stalk:** Indistinct, consisting of thickened area where branches are fused together; 1–3 cm wide; pinkish orange to pale red, sometimes white at the base; may be absent. **Spore Print:** Pale yellow. **Fruiting:** In scattered clusters on the ground under hemlock; fall. **Range:** West Coast; also reported from N.Y. **Family:** Clavariaceae. **Comments:** Some similar species cause gastric distress, so be certain of the identification. **Similar Species:** Yellow-tipped Coral (*R. formosa*; poisonous) is pinkish orange to light red, with yellow branch tips; it bruises brown. Clustered Coral (*R. botrytis*; edible, choice) is highly branched and white, with red to purple branch tips. Crown-tipped Coral (*Clavicorona pyxidata*; edible) has pale yellowish brown to pinkish tan branches with crown-like tips; it grows on decaying wood. *Clavulina cinerea* (edible) has pale gray to grayish brown branches; it grows on the ground. Crested Coral (*Clavulina cristata*; edible) has white to pale yellow branches with long, sharply pointed tips; it grows on the ground.

Rooting Cauliflower Mushroom, *Sparassis crispa*   EDIBLE, choice

Fruiting Body: 15–30 cm wide, 20–40 cm high; resembling leaf lettuce or cauliflower; composed of flattened, wrinkled, leaf-like branches; whitish to pale yellow. Flesh thin, fibrous, white. **Stalk:** 7–12 cm long, 2.5–4.5 cm thick, slightly narrowing toward the base; dark brown to black; tough; buried. **Spore Print:** White. **Fruiting:** Solitary or in groups on the ground or rotting wood in conifer forests; fall. **Range:** Pacific Northwest, south to the mountains of Ariz. **Family:** Clavariaceae. **Comments:** Previously known as *S. radicata*. The conspicuous cauliflower-like to lettuce-like appearance makes this mushroom easy to identify. **Similar Species:** Eastern Cauliflower Mushroom (*S. spathulata*, also known as *S. herbstii*; edible, choice; *see photo*) has wavy, cream to yellowish, leaf-like branches that are stiffer; it lacks a stalk.

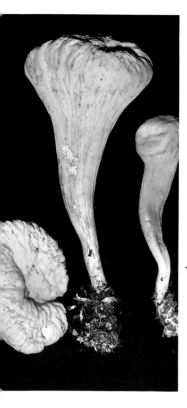

▲ Light Red Coral
Ramaria araiospora

◄ Flat-topped Coral
Clavariadelphus truncatus

Rooting
    Cauliflower Mushroom ▶
Sparassis crispa

Eastern
    Cauliflower Mushroom ▶
Sparassis spathulata

MORELS AND SIMILAR FUNGI

Ochre Jelly Club, *Leotia lubrica*   EDIBLE

Head: 1–3 cm wide; convex to nearly flat, with occasional grooves and a wavy, inrolled edge; surface smooth, slippery to gelatinous; pale yellow to olive brown. Flesh thick, gelatinous, pale yellow. **Stalk:** 2–6 cm long, 5–10 mm thick; nearly smooth, shiny, slippery; pale yellow to olive brown. **Spore Color:** White. **Fruiting:** Solitary, scattered, or fused in clusters on the ground in conifer and hardwood forests; summer, fall. **Range:** Throughout N. America. **Family:** Leotiaceae. **Comments:** Although edible, this mushroom is bland. **Similar Species:** Green-headed Jelly Club (*L. viscosa*; edibility unknown) has a green cap and a yellow to orange stalk. *L. atrovirens* (edibility unknown) has a green cap and stalk. Yellow Cudonia (*Cudonia lutea*; edibility unknown) has a yellowish orange cap and a yellow stalk; its texture is not gelatinous.

Round-headed Cordyceps, *Cordyceps capitata*   EDIBILITY UNKNOWN

Head: 5–20 mm wide; irregularly spherical; smooth, becoming minutely roughened from protruding tips of small, embedded, spore-containing flasks; moist to dry; brown to olive black. Flesh white. Odor not distinctive; taste mild. **Stalk:** 2–8 cm long, 5–15 mm thick, equal in thickness overall; smooth or slightly ridged; tough; dull yellow to olive brown. **Spore Color:** White (sometimes evident on head surface). **Fruiting:** Solitary or in small groups in woods, emerging from (and parasitic on) buried, walnut-shaped, finely warted, pale yellow fruiting bodies of *Elaphomyces* (a false truffle); summer, fall. **Range:** Throughout N. America. **Family:** Clavicipitaceae. **Comments:** The base must be dug up from below ground level to get the entire structure. **Similar Species:** Goldenthread Cordyceps (*C. ophioglossoides*; edibility unknown), which also grows from *Elaphomyces*, has a less distinct, cylindrical to tapered, reddish brown head.

Fluted Black Helvella, *Helvella lacunosa*   EDIBLE (caution)

Cap: 2–5 cm wide, 1–5 cm long; saddle-shaped to multi-lobed; wrinkled on the upper surface, smooth below; dark brown to gray to gray-black. Flesh brittle, gray. **Stalk:** 4–10 cm long, 1.5–2 cm thick; deeply ribbed; white to off white, often tinged grayish or yellowish brown; interior hollow, with chambers. **Spore Color:** White. **Fruiting:** Solitary or in groups in soil or on rotting wood; common in burned areas; fall to early winter. **Range:** Widely distributed in N. America. **Family:** Helvellaceae. **Comments:** Although this fungus is edible, some similar saddle-shaped species may be poisonous—a positive identification must be made. **Similar Species:** Fluted White Helvella (*H. crispa*; edible; *see photo*) has a white to pale cream cap and stalk. Smooth-stalked Helvella (*H. elastica*; edibility unknown) has a brown, saddle-shaped cap on a smooth, white to cream stalk. Long-stalked Gray Cup (*H. macropus*; edibility unknown) forms a gray cup on a slender, hairy, gray stalk.

▼ Ochre Jelly Club
Leotia lubrica

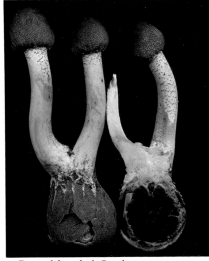

▲ Round-headed Cordyceps
on *Elaphomyces*
Cordyceps capitata

▲ Fluted White Helvella
Helvella crispa

◄ Fluted Black Helvella
Helvella lacunosa

MORELS AND SIMILAR FUNGI

Saddle-shaped False Morel, Gyromitra infula   POISONOUS

Cap: 5–10 cm wide, 2–10 cm long; saddle-shaped or multi-lobed; surface smooth to slightly wrinkled or folded; yellowish brown to reddish brown, aging to dark brown; interior hollow. Flesh thin, brittle, pinkish brown. **Stalk:** 3–9 cm long, 5–20 mm thick, equal in thickness overall or enlarging toward the base; sometimes with one or more grooves; white to grayish brown or pinkish brown. **Spore Color:** White. **Fruiting:** Solitary or in groups on the ground or on rotting wood; summer, fall. **Range:** Throughout N. America. **Family:** Helvellaceae. **Comments:** Because some species of Gyromitra are toxic, members of this genus are not recommended for consumption. **Similar Species:** G. ambigua (poisonous) has purple tints on both the cap and the stalk. Brown Bonnet (G. caroliniana; edible, caution; see photo) has a reddish brown cap with dense, irregular folds and numerous pit-like depressions; its white stalk has longitudinal ribs. Elephant Ears (G. fastigiata, also known as G. brunnea; poisonous) is less wrinkled and pitted. Both G. caroliniana and G. fastigiata are large and occur in Eastern N. America. Snow Mushroom (G. gigas; edible, caution) has fewer and broader folds, exhibits a brown to tan coloration throughout (without reddish shades), and has a shorter stalk; it is common in western N. America in late spring and early summer as the snow melts.

Smooth Thimble-cap, Verpa conica   EDIBLE

Cap: 1–2 cm wide, 1–3 cm long; conical to bell-shaped; smooth to slightly wrinkled; attached only at the tip of the stalk; brown, white on the undersurface. Flesh thin, brittle. **Stalk:** 3–6 cm long, 8–15 mm thick, nearly equal in thickness overall; white to yellowish white, with yellowish brown streaks; interior hollow. **Spore Color:** White to pale yellow. **Fruiting:** Solitary or in groups on the ground in hardwood forests (early spring) and under conifers at higher elevations as the winter snowpack melts (late spring to early summer). **Range:** Widely distributed in N. America. **Family:** Morchellaceae. **Comments:** This mushroom can often be found growing with morels in old apple orchards and other areas. **Similar Species:** Wrinkled Thimble-cap (V. bohemica; edible, choice) is larger and has a wrinkled, brown or yellowish brown cap.

Black Morel, Morchella elata   EDIBLE (caution)

Cap: 1–4.5 cm wide, 2.5–8 cm long, oval to conical; sponge-like, with dark brown to nearly black ridges surrounding irregular, yellow-brown to gray-brown pits. **Stalk:** 5–10 cm long, 1–4 cm thick, enlarged near the base; surface granular; interior hollow. **Spore Color:** Cream. **Fruiting:** Solitary or clustered on the ground in hardwood and conifer forests and burned areas; spring. **Range:** Throughout N. America. **Family:** Morchellaceae. **Comments:** Conical forms are also known as M. angusticeps. This is part of a complex of species that are difficult to separate. Although choice, it sometimes causes gastric distress when consumed with alcohol. **Similar Species:** Yellow Morel (M. esculenta; edible, choice) is nearly identical but has a pale yellow to yellow-brown cap. Half-free Morel (M. semilibera; edible, choice) has the lower half of its cap free (not attached to the stalk) and flaring. False Morel (Gyromitra esculenta; poisonous) and other Gyromitra species have a brain-like to wrinkled cap.

▲ Saddle-shaped False Morel
Gyromitra infula

Brown Bonnet ▶
Gyromitra caroliniana

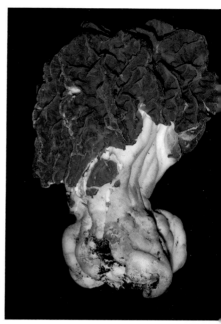

◀ Smooth Thimble-cap
Verpa conica

▼ Black Morel
Morchella elata

PUFFBALLS AND ALLIES

Devil's Snuffbox, *Lycoperdon perlatum*   EDIBLE, choice (caution)

Fruiting Body: 2.5–5 cm wide, 2.5–8 cm tall; pear-shaped to turban-shaped; surface covered with numerous short, pyramidal spines of two sizes; white at first, aging to yellow-brown. Flesh solid and white when young, aging to yellow, then olive brown and powdery. **Spore Color:** Olive brown. **Fruiting:** Solitary or in groups on mulch, compost piles, or the ground in conifer and hardwood forests; summer, fall (also winter in the South). **Range:** Throughout N. America. **Family:** Lycoperdaceae. **Comments:** Also known as Gem-studded Puffball. Edible when the interior is pure white. Discard those that have started to change color; old specimens may cause gastric distress. **Similar Species:** Pear-shaped Puffball (*L. pyriforme*; edible if internally pure white) has a smoother-looking surface (feels like sandpaper) and grows in clusters—often in large numbers—on decaying wood.

Pigskin Poison Puffball, *Scleroderma citrinum*   POISONOUS

Fruiting Body: 2.5–8 cm wide, 1–4 cm tall; oval to round; yellow-brown, covered with raised, yellow-brown warts on a polygonal background. Rind thick. Flesh white at first, quickly turning purple-black to black with white marbling; powdery at maturity. **Stalk:** Short, thick, and irregularly shaped; may be absent. **Spore Color:** Purple-black. **Fruiting:** Solitary, scattered, or clustered on the ground under conifers or hardwoods; summer, fall. **Range:** Widely distributed in eastern N. America. **Family:** Sclerodermataceae. **Comments:** Known as *S. aurantium* in some works. The thick, tough outer covering splits open to release the spores. Some species of *Scleroderma* are known to cause gastric distress. Parasitic Bolete (*Boletus parasiticus*; edible) sometimes grows attached to the base of this puffball. **Similar Species:** *Scleroderma areolatum* (poisonous) is much smaller and has numerous dot-like surface scales and a thinner rind.

Purple-spored Puffball, *Calvatia cyathiformis*   EDIBLE, choice (caution)

Fruiting Body: 7–16 cm wide, 9–20 cm high; round, oval, or skull-shaped. Outer surface smooth, white to pale brown, breaking into thin, irregular plates that flake off with age. Flesh solid and white at first, aging to yellowish and finally purple-brown and powdery. **Stalk:** Thick, short, anchored by thick strands; interior spongy. **Spore Color:** Purple-brown. **Fruiting;** Solitary or scattered in grassy areas and at woodland edges; late summer, fall. **Range:** Widely distributed in N. America. **Family:** Lycoperdaceae. **Comments:** Edible if interior is white; reported to cause gastric distress once the interior begins to change color. **Similar Species:** Skull-shaped Puffball (*C. craniformis*) is nearly identical but has a yellow-olive, powdery interior at maturity. Giant Puffball (*C. gigantea*) can grow to 50 cm wide, lacks a stalk, and is white, with an interior that ages to yellowish brown. Both are edible and choice if the interior is white.

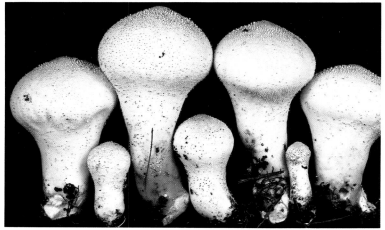

▲ Devil's Snuffbox
Lycoperdon perlatum

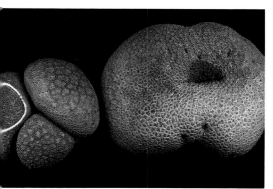

▲ Pigskin Poison Puffball
Scleroderma citrinum

Purple-spored Puffball ▶
Calvatia cyathiformis

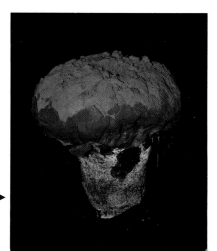

PUFFBALLS AND ALLIES

Pyramid Puffball, *Calvatia sculpta*   EDIBLE (caution)

Fruiting Body: 5–15 cm wide, 6–15 cm tall; when young, covered with coarse, erect (*see photo*) or bent-over spines; upon aging, spines split vertically but remain fused at the tips (*see photo*); spines bear parallel horizontal lines toward the base; surface white. Flesh solid and white at first, aging to olive brown and powdery. **Stalk:** Up to 7 cm wide and 7 cm long; tapered to short and cylindrical; interior sponge-like, often purplish. **Spore Color:** Yellow-brown to olive-brown. **Fruiting:** Solitary or scattered in humus under conifers at high elevations; summer, fall. **Range:** Western N. America, especially the Pacific Northwest. **Family:** Lycoperdaceae. **Comments:** This distinctive fungus is edible when the interior is white. **Similar Species:** Sculptured Puffball (*Calbovista subsculpta*) is covered with low pyramidal warts. The golf ball-sized Alpine Puffball (*Calvatia subcretacea*) is covered with small, white scales that are tipped with gray-brown; it has a thick rind. Both species are edible when the interior is pure white.

Dye-maker's False Puffball, *Pisolithus tinctorius*   INEDIBLE

Fruiting Body: 5–11 cm wide, 5–20 cm high, irregularly spherical, pear-shaped, or club-shaped, usually tapered; smooth to slightly roughened; yellow-brown, with brownish black spots in mature specimens. Rind thin. Flesh containing numerous, egg-shaped compartments, each surrounded by a dark, gelatinous wall when young; compartments becoming brown and powdery with maturity; maturation sequential from the apex to the base. **Stalk:** Present as a tapering base; interior fibrous. **Spore Color:** Brown. **Fruiting:** Solitary or scattered in mixed woods, near trees or shrubs in disturbed areas (gardens, trails, road cuts), and in soils of marginal quality; summer, fall. **Range:** Widely distributed in N. America. **Family:** Sclerodermataceae. **Comments:** Sometimes used as a source of brown and black dyes. **Similar Species:** No other species with powdery spores has the compartmentalized interior at maturity.

Geastrum fimbriatum   EDIBILITY UNKNOWN

Fruiting Body: Spherical and up to 2 cm wide before opening; up to 7 cm wide at maturity; outer layer splitting to form 5–10 radiating, tapered, pallid, smooth-surfaced rays and exposing a spherical inner spore case nestled in a bowl-like depression of fused ray bases; spore sac 8–15 mm wide, spherical, with a shaggy mouth at the apex. **Stalk:** Absent. **Spore Color:** Dark brown. **Fruiting:** Scattered or in groups under hardwoods; fall. **Range:** Widely distributed throughout N. America. **Family:** Geastraceae. **Comments:** This is one of several species known as earthstars. Before opening, earthstars resemble other puffballs, but the multilayered nature and more rubbery texture of their outer layers are easily seen when they are cut in half. **Similar Species:** Rounded Earthstar (*G. saccatum;* edibility unknown) has a distinct circular ridge or depression separating the mouth area from the rest of the spore case. In the Collared Earthstar (*G. triplex;* edibility unknown) the spore sac sits in a free-edged bowl formed by the separation of adjacent inner layers from the rest of the ray tissue.

Pyramid Puffball (young) ▶
Calvatia sculpta

▼ Pyramid Puffball (old)
Calvatia sculpta

Dye-maker's
False Puffball ▶
*Pisolithus
tinctorius*

▼ *Geastrum fimbriatum*

JELLY AND JELLY-LIKE FUNGI

Apricot Jelly, *Phlogiotis helvelloides*   EDIBLE

Fruiting Body: 2–6 cm wide, 2.5–8 cm tall; tongue-shaped to spoon-shaped; smooth, gelatinous; pinkish red to apricot-colored. Undersurface slightly roughened, pale pinkish red. Flesh thin, gelatinous to rubbery, grayish white. **Stalk:** Short, off-center, becoming narrower at the base; continuous with upper part of the fruiting body; smooth; pinkish red to apricot. **Spore Print:** White. **Fruiting:** Solitary or in groups on the ground or rotting wood in conifer and mixed forests; spring, summer, fall. **Range:** Widely distributed in N. America. **Family:** Tremellaceae. **Comments:** Although edible, this mushroom is rather bland. It is sometimes candied. **Similar Species:** Jelly Tooth (*Pseudohydnum gelatinosum;* edible) is translucent white, has spines on the lower surface, and grows on rotting wood and woody debris on the forest floor.

Orange Jelly, *Dacrymyces palmatus*   EDIBLE

Fruiting Body: 1–6 cm wide, 1–2 cm high; a multi-lobed mass of yellowish orange to orange tissue; white near the point of attachment; gelatinous, shrinking, and becoming hard when dry. Flesh thin, gelatinous, and soft when fresh. **Stalk:** Absent. **Spore Color:** White. **Fruiting:** In clusters on fallen branches and logs of conifers; year-round. **Range:** Throughout N. America. **Family:** Dacrymycetaceae. **Comments:** Also known as Orange Witches' Butter. This fungus has a rather bland taste and may be eaten raw or cooked. **Similar Species:** Witches' Butter (*Tremella mesenterica;* edible) is yellow-orange and grows on hardwood logs and fallen branches. Yellow Witches' Butter (*T. lutescens;* edible) is pale yellow, smaller, and more lobed.

Ductifera pululahuana   EDIBILITY UNKNOWN

Fruiting Body: 8–30 mm wide, up to 2 cm tall; more or less hemispherical, irregularly folded to brain-like, sometimes multi-lobed, enlarging and fusing to form elongated, irregular masses; flesh thin; entire fruiting body firm and waxy, but becoming soft and gelatinous when old or very wet; white to cream; shrinking, becoming hard, and turning to cream to olive brown on drying. **Stalk:** Absent. **Spore Print:** White. **Fruiting:** On rotten wood, usually barkless logs; summer, fall. **Range:** Eastern N. America. **Family:** Tremellaceae. **Comments:** Easily distinguished from other jelly fungi by the combination of its color, form, and the material on which it grows (substrate). **Similar Species:** *Sebacina concrescens* (edibility unknown) is similar in color, form, and texture, but it fruits on the ground around the bases of upright herbaceous plants, including poison ivy.

▲ Apricot Jelly
Phlogiotis helvelloides

Orange Jelly ▶
Dacrymyces palmatus

▼ *Ductifera pululahuana*

JELLY AND JELLY-LIKE FUNGI

Black Jelly Roll, *Exidia glandulosa*   EDIBLE

Fruiting Body: 1–2 cm wide, up to 1 cm high; gland-like to blister-like, in long irregular rows up to 20 cm long; soft, gelatinous; reddish brown to black. Flesh thin, gelatinous, watery. **Stalk:** Absent. **Spore Color:** White. **Fruiting:** In large clusters on hardwood logs and fallen branches; spring, summer, fall. **Range:** Throughout N. America. **Family:** Tremellaceae. **Comments:** Also known as Black Witches' Butter. Although listed as edible, this species is bland. **Similar species:** Granular Jelly Roll (*E. nucleata;* edibility unknown; *see photo*) is white, aging to yellowish brown to reddish brown; it has small, white, seed-like structures embedded inside the gelatinous lobes. Pale Jelly Roll (*E. alba;* edibility unknown) is white to very pale yellowish, even when old.

Silver Ear, *Tremella fuciformis*   EDIBILITY UNKNOWN

Fruiting Body: Up to 8 cm across and 4 cm tall; silvery translucent; composed of numerous upright, irregularly shaped, lobed, flattened, and sac-like branches fused in a net-like pattern toward the base; each branch up to 4.5 cm wide, rounded at the edges; branches more or less flaccid, gelatinous to rubbery; shrinking, becoming very hard, and turning dull cream to pale olive brown on drying; interior hollow. Flesh thin. **Stalk:** Absent. **Fruiting:** Solitary or scattered on dead hardwood branches and logs; summer, fall. **Range:** Southeastern U.S., north to southern Ill. **Family:** Tremellaceae. **Comments:** In Asia, the local form of this species is grown commercially, but the edibility of material growing in N. America is not documented. **Similar Species:** *T. reticulata* (edibility unknown), a northeastern and northern north-central species, is white to pale cream (not translucent) and irregularly branched; it exhibits a net-like pattern below the branches.

Tree Ear, *Auricularia auricula*   EDIBLE

Fruiting Body: 3–15 cm wide; ear-shaped or irregularly cup-shaped; rubbery to gelatinous; undersurface smooth, reddish brown to purplish brown; upper surface wrinkled, minutely hairy to velvety, reddish brown. Flesh thin, gelatinous to rubbery. **Stalk:** Absent. **Spore Print:** White. **Fruiting:** Solitary, in groups, or in fused clusters on logs and standing stumps; spring, summer, fall. **Range:** Throughout N. America. **Family:** Auriculariaceae. **Comments:** Cut into small pieces, this mushroom is commonly added to soups and stews as a flavoring and is very similar to one grown commercially in China. **Similar Species:** Amber Jelly Roll (*Exidia recisa;* edibility unknown) is cushion-shaped to irregularly wrinkled, has a very short stalk, and is yellowish brown to reddish brown.

Black Jelly Roll ▶
Exidia glandulosa

▼ Granular Jelly Roll
Exidia nucleata

▼ Tree Ear
Auricularia auricula

▼ Silver Ear
Tremella fuciformis

SMOOTH AND CRUST FUNGI

Trembling Merulius, *Phlebia tremellosa*   EDIBILITY UNKNOWN

Fruiting Body: 2–8 cm wide, 5–10 cm high; a spreading to circular mass of overlapping tissue. Outer (lower) surface with radiating to wrinkled ridges and crossveins; often forming pore-like depressions in more mature specimens; yellowish orange to pinkish orange. Upper surface and edges hairy to nearly smooth, white to pale yellow. Flesh thick, gelatinous, white to yellow. **Stalk:** Absent. **Spore Print:** White. **Fruiting:** In clusters on stumps and logs, often emerging from beneath the soil line; summer, fall. **Range:** Throughout N. America. **Family:** Corticaceae. **Comments:** Also known as *Merulius tremellosus*. Although its undersurface sometimes forms pore-like depressions, this species lacks the regular tubes and leathery to woody texture of polypores. **Similar Species:** Radiating Phlebia (*P. radiata;* edibility unknown) has pinkish to orange-red, radiating folds or wrinkles; its undersurface never develops pore-like depressions.

Silky Parchment, *Stereum striatum*   INEDIBLE

Fruiting Body: 5–15 mm wide; fan-shaped, attached by a narrow base. Upper surface of radiating, silky, grayish white fibers and pale brown zones. Undersurface smooth, white to pale yellowish brown. Flesh very thin, white. **Stalk:** Reduced or absent. **Spore Print:** White. **Fruiting:** Solitary, scattered, or in overlapping groups on dead hardwood branches; year-round. **Range:** Eastern N. America, west to the Great Plains states. **Family:** Stereaceae. **Comments:** Also called *S. sericeum.* Species in this family resemble small polypores but lack tiny pores on the undersurface. **Similar Species:** False Turkey-tail (*S. ostrea;* inedible) is larger, with multicolored zones of brown to reddish brown on the upper surface and yellow-orange to yellow-brown coloration on the undersurface. Hairy Parchment (*S. hirsutum;* inedible) is yellow-brown or gray, has reddish brown zones, and is covered with dense, short, stiff hairs.

Ceramic Parchment, *Xylobolus frustulatus*   INEDIBLE

Fruiting Body: 5–25 mm wide; a crust-like layer of many-sided plates resembling broken pieces of dull ceramic tile, fused into irregular patches; pinkish white to reddish brown when young, older specimens tan to grayish tan. Flesh up to 1 mm thick, very hard, whitish. **Stalk:** Absent. **Spore Color:** White. **Fruiting:** In clusters up to 15 cm wide on barkless hardwood stumps and logs; year-round. **Range:** Widely distributed throughout N. America. **Family:** Stereaceae. **Comments:** A distinctive species often found on dead oak and more common in the East. **Similar Species:** Two-tone Parchment (*Laxitextum bicolor;* inedible) has a spongy, pliant fruiting body and coffee-colored upper surface. Hophornbeam Disc (*Aleurodiscus oakesii;* inedible) is thinner, more regularly disc-shaped, and fleshy to leathery.

▲ Trembling Merulius
Phlebia tremellosa

Silky Parchment ▶
Stereum striatum

▼ Ceramic Parchment
Xylobolus frustulatus

SPINE FUNGI

Pine Cone Fungus, *Auriscalpium vulgare*   INEDIBLE

Cap: 1–4 cm wide; semicircular to kidney-shaped in outline, broadly convex to flattened; cap edge even, wavy, or lobed, often with a hairy fringe; dry, densely hairy; pale to dark brown. Undersurface covered with spines (teeth; *see photo*) 2–3 mm long, cream to nearly flesh-colored at first, becoming dark brown (sometimes tinged violet) at maturity. Flesh thin, leathery, white to light brown. **Stalk:** 2.5–7.5 cm long, 1–3 mm thick, widening toward the base; tough and pliant; densely hairy; dark reddish brown to brown; attached at the side of the cap (rarely central). **Spore Print:** White. **Fruiting:** Solitary or in groups on pine and Douglas-fir cones and cone debris on the ground; late summer, fall. **Range:** Throughout N. America. **Family:** Hydnaceae. **Comments:** A dainty but distinctive fungus. **Similar Species:** None.

Bearded Tooth, *Hericium erinaceus*   EDIBLE, choice

Fruiting Body: 8–25 cm wide, 6–20 cm high; consisting of spines (teeth) 1–4 cm long, pointing out and downward from a solid mass at the point of attachment; white to dull yellow. Flesh thick, fibrous, white; forming a thick base. **Stalk:** Absent. **Spore Print:** White. **Fruiting:** Solitary on live trees, dead logs, and stumps; late summer, fall. **Range:** Throughout N. America. **Family:** Hydnaceae. **Comments:** Also known as the Hedgehog Mushroom, it is excellent in soups and stews (especially young specimens). **Similar Species:** *H. erinaceus* ssp. *erinaceo-abietis* (edible; *see photo*) has small, short, white spines covering the entire surface of the fruiting body; it is found on hardwood logs and stumps in summer and fall in the Southeast and southern Midwest.

▲ Pine Cone Fungus (cap)
Auriscalpium vulgare

Pine Cone Fungus ▶
(teeth)
Auriscalpium vulgare

▲ Bearded Tooth
Hericium erinaceus

Hericium erinaceus
ssp. *erinaceo-abietis* ▶

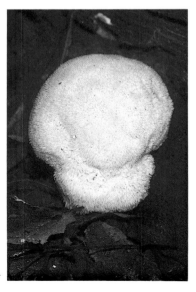

SPINE FUNGI

Comb Tooth, *Hericium coralloides*   EDIBLE, choice

Fruiting Body: 7–25 cm wide, 7–20 cm tall; a cluster of comb-like branches; smooth; white to dull yellow with age. Undersides of branches lined with spines (teeth) 5–25 mm long. Flesh soft, thick, watery when fresh, white. **Stalk:** Absent. **Spore Print:** White. **Fruiting:** In clusters hanging on decaying stumps and logs of hardwoods; summer, fall. **Range:** Throughout N. America. **Family:** Hydnaceae. **Comments:** Previously known as *H. ramosum.* Also called Icicle. **Similar Species:** Bear's Head Tooth (*H. americanum;* formerly known in N. America as *H. coralloides*) and *H. abietis* (both edible and choice) are similar but have the spines in clusters at the branch tips (not lining the undersides); *H. americanum* occurs on hardwood stumps and logs in the East, and *H. abietis* grows on dead conifer wood in the West. Bearded Tooth (*H. erinaceus;* edible, choice) is an unbranched, white to yellowish mass of long spines.

Sweet Tooth, *Hydnum repandum*   EDIBLE, choice

Cap: 2–10 cm wide; convex to nearly flat or slightly depressed in the center; smooth to slightly roughened; cap edge even to wavy; yellowish orange or pale orange to brownish orange. Undersurface covered with cream-colored spines (teeth) 3–8 mm long. Flesh thick, brittle, white to pale yellow. **Stalk:** 2–8 cm long, 1–3 cm thick; occasionally off-center; smooth; cream white to colored like the cap; interior solid. **Spore Print:** White. **Fruiting:** Solitary or scattered on the ground under conifers and hardwoods; summer, fall. **Range:** Throughout N. America. **Family:** Hydnaceae. **Comments:** Also known as *Dentinum repandum.* Reminiscent of a small chanterelle until the lower surface is examined. **Similar Species:** *H. umbilicatum* (edible) is smaller and darker, has a sunken cap center, and occurs in wet conifer woods. Scaly Tooth (*H. imbricatum;* edible) has brown spines, a brown hollow stalk, and a coarsely scaly, brown cap. *H. scabrosum* is nearly identical to the Scaly Tooth, but it has a black stalk base and a bitter taste.

Jelly False Tooth, *Pseudohydnum gelatinosum*   EDIBLE

Cap: 1–6 cm wide; fan-shaped, convex to nearly flat; smooth or with very short, fine hairs; moist; translucent white with a dull pearl gray to grayish brown cast. Undersurface covered with short, shaggy, white spines (teeth). Flesh gelatinous, translucent white. **Stalk:** Up to 5 cm long, broader and flatter above; attached at the side of the cap; smooth; translucent white; often absent if attached at the side of a log. **Spore Print:** White. **Fruiting:** Solitary or in groups on conifer twigs and logs on the ground in cool, wet conditions; spring, fall. **Range:** Throughout N. America. **Family:** Tremellaceae. **Comments:** Also known as White Jelly Mushroom. Can be eaten raw with sugar and cream, marinated for salads, or candied and dusted with sugar. **Similar Species:** Apricot Jelly (*Phlogiotis helvelloides;* edible) is somewhat similar in form but is apricot-colored and lacks teeth.

◀ Comb Tooth
Hericium coralloides

▼ Sweet Tooth
Hydnum repandum

▼ Jelly False Tooth
Pseudohydnum gelatinosum

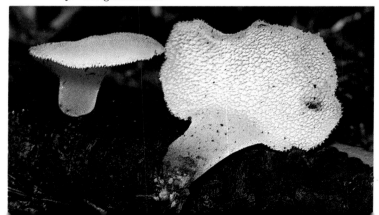

POLYPORES AND ALLIES

Turkey-tail, *Coriolus versicolor*   INEDIBLE

Caps: Each 2–5 cm wide; semicircular; leathery. Upper surface velvety to nearly smooth, with variously colored linear zones (white, yellow, brown, bluish, orange, red). Undersurface white, with many small pores. Flesh less than 3 mm thick, white. **Stalk:** Absent. **Spore Print:** White. **Fruiting:** Solitary to overlapping or sometimes in fused clusters on dead wood; summer, fall. **Range:** Throughout N. America. **Family:** Polyporaceae. **Comments:** Very common. Inedible because of its tough texture. A hand lens may be needed to see the pores. **Similar Species:** False Turkey-tail (*Stereum ostrea*; inedible) also has colored zones but is more narrowly fan-shaped; it lacks pores on the lower surface. Smoky Polypore (*Bjerkandera adusta*; inedible) has a smoky gray to nearly white upper surface and grayish pores that bruise black.

Cinnabar Red Polypore, *Pycnoporus cinnabarinus*   INEDIBLE

Cap: 2–12 cm wide; fan-shaped, flat to slightly convex. Upper surface roughened, red to reddish orange, fading to dull pale orange; cap edge thin, wavy. Undersurface with pores, red, fading to reddish orange or yellowish orange. Flesh moderately thick, firm, reddish orange to yellow-orange. **Stalk:** Absent. **Spore Print:** Cream white. **Fruiting:** Solitary, scattered, or in overlapping clusters on hardwood logs and stumps; year-round. **Range:** Widely distributed in N. America. **Family:** Polyporaceae. **Comments:** Common on charred wood after forest fires. **Similar Species:** *P. sanguineus* (inedible) has a much thinner, smooth, and slightly darker cap and is more southern in distribution. Beefsteak Polypore (*Fistulina hepatica*; edible) is larger and fleshy; it has a dark, dull reddish (meat red) cap and cream to reddish brown pores.

Violet Toothed Polypore, *Trichaptum biformis*   INEDIBLE

Caps: Each 1–6 cm wide; semicircular, nearly flat. Upper surface hairy, white to grayish, sometimes with variously colored linear zones (brown, reddish brown, purple-brown; also greenish if covered with algae), especially toward the cap edge. Undersurface composed of angular pores that often rupture vertically and become irregularly tooth-like; purple-brown to purple (especially along the edge), fading to white with age. Flesh thin, fibrous, white. **Stalk:** Absent. **Spore Print:** White. **Fruiting:** In overlapping clusters on dead hardwoods; year-round. **Range:** Throughout N. America. **Family:** Polyporaceae. **Comments:** Also known as *Hirschioporus pargamenus*. **Similar Species:** *Trichaptum abietinus* (inedible; *see photo*) is smaller, has stiff white hairs on the cap, and grows on conifer wood.

▲ Turkey-tail
Coriolus versicolor

Cinnabar Red Polypore ▶
Pycnoporus cinnabarinus

◀ Violet Toothed Polypore
Trichaptum biformis

▼ *Trichaptum abietinus*

POLYPORES AND ALLIES

Birch Polypore, *Piptoporus betulinus* EDIBLE

Cap: 3–25 cm wide; shell-shaped to kidney-shaped, convex to nearly flat; cap edge inrolled. Upper surface smooth, pale brown with dark brown streaks. Undersurface composed of white to pale yellowish brown pores. Flesh thick, firm, white. **Stalk:** Absent, or present only as a thickened attachment point. **Spore Print:** White. **Fruiting:** Solitary, scattered, or in overlapping groups on living or dead birch trees; year-round. **Range:** Eastern N. America (reported from Wash.). **Family:** Polyporaceae. **Comments:** Young specimens can be sliced into small pieces and fried in butter; older ones are too woody. **Similar Species:** Dryad's Saddle (*Polyporus squamosus*; edible) has a stubby lateral stalk and a yellowish brown, kidney-shaped cap covered with dense brown scales; it grows on decaying hardwood trees and stumps. Veiled Polypore (*Cryptoporus volvatus*; inedible) grows on conifers and has a round to kidney-shaped, stalkless fruiting body; the pores are covered over by a thick, veil-like membrane.

Hexagonal-pored Polypore, *Favolus alveolaris* EDIBLE

Cap: 1–8 cm wide; broadly fan-shaped. Upper surface reddish yellow to reddish brown with darker scales, fading to pale yellow with age. Undersurface with large, angular, white to pale yellow pores. Flesh thin, fibrous, white. **Stalk:** Short, off-center; pores extending to the base; stalk sometimes absent. **Spore Print:** White. **Fruiting:** Solitary or scattered on dead hardwood branches; spring to fall. **Range:** Eastern N. America, west to the Rocky Mountains. **Family:** Polyporaceae. **Comments:** Although edible, it is usually too fibrous and tough to be eaten. **Similar Species:** Spring Polypore (*Polyporus arcularius*; inedible) has a scaly, circular brown cap; Winter Polypore (*P. brumalis*; inedible) has a smooth, circular, grayish brown to brownish black cap. Both have a central stalk and grow on dead hardwood. Dryad's Saddle (*P. squamosus*; edible) is larger, with a yellow-brown cap and dark brown scales, white to yellowish angular pores, and a thick, off-center stalk; it grows on decaying hardwood trees and stumps.

Artist's Conk, *Ganoderma applanatum* INEDIBLE

Cap: 5–60 cm wide; convex to hoof-shaped. Upper surface dull, greenish gray, reddish brown, gray-brown, or grayish black, with hard zones that frequently crack (often covered with dull reddish brown spores). Undersurface white to cream white (bruising brown), with minute pores. Flesh thick, soft, white in young specimens, aging to brown; downwardly directed tubes are layered; both flesh and tubes harden with age. **Stalk:** Absent. **Spore Print:** Reddish brown. **Fruiting:** Solitary, scattered, or in overlapping clusters on hardwoods (occasionally conifers); year-round. **Range:** Throughout N. America. **Family:** Polyporaceae. **Comments:** Often used by artists, who etch pictures on the lower surface with knives or other sharp objects. **Similar Species:** Hemlock Varnish Shelf (*G. tsugae*; inedible; *see photo*) grows on conifers in northern parts of eastern N. America, and *G. oregonense* (inedible) occurs on conifers in the Pacific Northwest; both are shiny (appear varnished), fan-shaped to kidney-shaped, and reddish brown, and both have white flesh. Ling Chih (*G. lucidum*; inedible), nearly identical to these two, and the southern, more yellow *G. curtisii* (inedible) have light brown flesh and grow on hardwoods. Red-belted Polypore (*Fomitopsis pinicola*; inedible) is hoof-shaped and grayish brown, with a yellow-orange to dull red outer zone, pores that are white to cream, and layered tubes. Conifer-base Polypore (*Heterobasidion annosum*; inedible) has grayish brown to brownish black zones, a wavy cap edge, white pores, and white flesh.

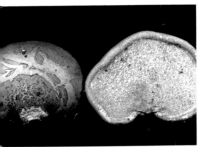

▲ Birch Polypore
Piptoporus betulinus

▲ Hexagonal-pored Polypore
Favolus alveolaris

Artist's Conk ▶
Ganoderma applanatum

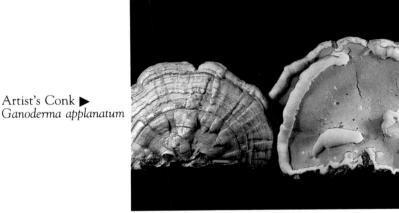

▼ Hemlock Varnish Shelf
Ganoderma tsugae

POLYPORES AND ALLIES

Beefsteak Polypore, *Fistulina hepatica*   EDIBLE

Cap: 8–25 cm wide; semicircular, slightly convex to nearly flat. Upper surface slightly roughened to nearly smooth, gelatinous, reddish orange to dark red (the color of raw beef). Undersurface composed of numerous yellowish brown to reddish brown pores. Flesh thick, juicy-gelatinous, pinkish red. **Stalk:** Thick, short, same color as the cap; sometimes absent. **Spore Print:** Pinkish salmon to pale orange-brown. **Fruiting:** Solitary or scattered at the bases of living oak trees and on oak stumps and logs; summer, fall. **Range:** Widely distributed; most common in southeastern N. America. **Family:** Polyporaceae. **Comments:** The species name *hepatica* means liver; it refers to the cap color and shape of this excellent edible. **Similar Species:** Resinous Polypore (*Ischnoderma resinosum;* inedible) is semicircular, flattened, velvety, juicy, and yellowish brown to dark reddish brown.

Hen of the Woods, *Grifola frondosa*   EDIBLE, choice

Caps: Each 2–8 cm wide; more or less fan-shaped. Upper surface smooth or nearly so, gray to grayish brown. Undersurface white to pale yellow, with numerous tiny pores. Flesh thick, firm, white. Grows in massive clusters up to 60 cm wide and weighing 5 to 10 pounds or more. **Stalk:** Large, highly branched, white; fused at the base and extending upward to support overlapping clusters of caps. **Spore Print:** White. **Fruiting:** Solitary or scattered on the ground, usually near the bases of trees or stumps; summer, fall. **Range:** Eastern N. America and the Pacific Northwest. **Family:** Polyporaceae. **Comments:** Usually fruits in the same place for several years. **Similar Species:** Umbrella Polypore (*Polyporus umbellatus;* edible) forms large clusters of round, centrally attached, white to tan caps with pores that descend down the highly branched stalk. Black-staining Polypore (*Meripilus giganteus;* edible) has many thick, fan-shaped, grayish yellow caps with creamy white pores that bruise black; the branched stalk is short and thick.

Sulphur Shelf, *Laetiporus sulphureus*   EDIBLE (caution)

Caps: Each 5–30 cm wide, up to 2.5 cm thick; fan-shaped to semicircular, flattened. Upper surface suede-like, wrinkled to lumpy, bright to dull orange, fading to dull yellow or chalky white; cap edge thick, wavy, bright to pale yellow. Undersurface with numerous small pores, bright sulphur yellow, fading to pale yellow. Flesh succulent when young, aging to tough, then dry and crumbly; white. **Stalk:** Absent. **Spore Print:** White to buff. **Fruiting:** Solitary or more commonly in closely overlapping clusters on logs, stumps, and standing trees; summer, fall, occasionally spring. **Range:** Throughout N. America. **Family:** Polyporaceae. **Comments:** Commonly called Chicken of the Woods. Will fruit from the same log for several years. Reports of poisoning in the West may be related to the material (substrate) on which it grows: it may cause gastrointestinal upset when growing on *Eucalyptus* and at least some conifers; use caution. **Similar Species:** *L. semialbinus* (edible) is also orange but bears a stalk and has a white lower surface with pores; it grows from the ground (on buried wood).

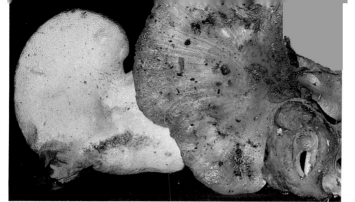

▲ Beefsteak Polypore
Fistulina hepatica

▲ Hen of the Woods
Grifola frondosa

▼ Sulphur Shelf
Laetiporus sulphureus

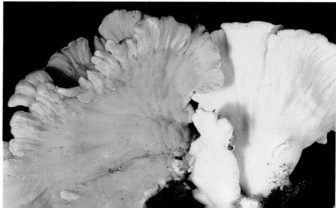

BOLETES

Ash-tree Bolete, *Boletinellus merulioides* EDIBLE

Cap: 5–15 cm wide; convex to nearly flat, sometimes slightly depressed in the center; smooth, with a wavy edge; yellowish brown, reddish brown, or olive brown. Undersurface composed of radially elongated pores that sometimes appear vein-like; bright yellow, yellowish brown with age. Flesh pale yellow, slowly staining bluish green; taste mild to bitter. **Stalk:** 2–5 cm long, 5–25 mm thick; off-center; yellowish brown to reddish brown; interior solid. **Spore Print:** Olive brown. **Fruiting:** Solitary, scattered, or in groups on the ground under hardwoods, especially ash; summer, fall. **Range:** Eastern N. America, west to Minn. and Mo. **Family:** Boletaceae. **Comments:** Also known as *Gyrodon merulioides.* This mushroom is frequently eaten by deer and other animals but is not avidly collected for the table. **Similar Species:** *Boletus modestus* (edibility unknown) is similar but has a yellowish brown to reddish brown cap, a centrally attached stalk, and elongated gill-like pores; it is not common.

Chestnut Bolete, *Gyroporus castaneus* EDIBLE, choice

Cap: 3–12 cm wide; convex, aging to flat; dry, smooth, minutely velvety; pale orange-brown to chestnut brown. Undersurface composed of numerous small pores; white, aging to yellow. Flesh soft, white. **Stalk:** 3–9 cm long, 6–22 mm thick, sometimes enlarged toward the base; smooth; orange-brown to pale chestnut brown; interior cottony to hollow, white. **Spore Print:** Yellow. **Fruiting:** Solitary, scattered, or in groups in soil under hardwoods and in mixed forests; summer, fall. **Range:** Throughout eastern N. America, west to Minn., Mo., and Ariz.; rare in central Calif. **Family:** Boletaceae. **Comments:** Small but worthwhile if collected in quantity. **Similar Species:** Red Gyroporus (*G. purpurinus;* edible) has a deep burgundy red cap. Bluing Bolete (*G. cyanescens;* edible) has a paler cap and stalk, and all parts quickly turn blue when bruised. These two species also form yellow spore prints.

Zeller's Bolete, *Boletus zelleri* EDIBLE

Cap: 5–12 cm wide; convex to nearly flat; dry, velvety, and somewhat wrinkled, becoming nearly smooth with age; grayish black to brownish black when young, becoming olive brown to brown in older specimens. Undersurface composed of many small pores, bright yellow to olive yellow, bruising blue. Flesh firm, thick, cream to pale yellow, sometimes slowly bruising blue. **Stalk:** 5–12 cm long, 5–20 mm thick, nearly equal in thickness overall; smooth to somewhat granular; yellow (and often with red granules) when young, aging to yellowish red and finally dark red. **Spore Print:** Olive brown. **Fruiting:** Solitary, scattered, or in small groups on the ground under conifers, including redwood; fall. **Range:** Pacific Northwest into Calif. **Family:** Boletaceae. **Comments:** Formerly known as *Xerocomus zelleri.* **Similar Species:** Red-cracked Bolete (*Boletus chrysenteron;* edible) has an olive brown cap that cracks, exposing flesh that ages to pinkish red. *Boletellus chrysenteroides* (edibility unknown), found only in eastern N. America, has a velvety to smooth, dark reddish brown, cracked cap with pale exposed flesh.

Ash-tree Bolete ▶
Boletinellus merulioides

▲ Chestnut Bolete
Gyroporus castaneus

Zeller's Bolete ▶
Boletus zelleri

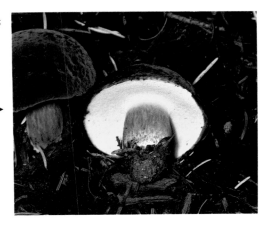

BOLETES

Violet-Gray Bolete, *Tylopilus plumbeoviolaceus* INEDIBLE

Cap: 4–15 cm wide; convex to nearly flat; dry, velvety; dull violet when young, aging to grayish violet to dull cinnamon brown. Undersurface composed of small pores, cream-colored, becoming pinkish to pinkish brown in mature specimens. Flesh thick, white; taste bitter. **Stalk:** 8–12 cm long, 1–1.7 cm thick, sometimes enlarged below; smooth or with slightly raised, net-like ridges at the apex; violet in young specimens, becoming paler and browner with age; paler at the base; interior solid, white. **Spore Print:** Pinkish brown. **Fruiting:** Solitary, scattered, or in groups under hardwoods, especially oak and hickory; summer, fall. **Range:** Eastern N. America, west to Minn. and Ariz. **Family:** Boletaceae. **Comments:** Older specimens are sometimes hard to identify because the violet coloration fades. **Similar Species:** *T. rubrobrunneus* (edibility unknown) is also bitter but lacks the violet to lilac coloration.

Bitter Bolete, *Tylopilus felleus* INEDIBLE

Cap: 6–30 cm wide; convex to broadly convex; tacky when wet, nearly smooth when dry; light to dark brown. Undersurface composed of many small pores, white when young, aging to pink and bruising brown. Flesh thick, soft, white, turning slightly pink where bruised; taste very bitter. **Stalk:** 4–12 cm long, 1–2.5 cm thick, enlarged toward the base; dry; light brown with raised, net-like ridges over nearly its entire length. **Spore Print:** Pink to pinkish brown. **Fruiting:** Solitary to scattered on the ground under conifers and hardwoods; summer, fall. **Range:** Eastern N. America, west to Mich., Mo., and Ariz. **Family:** Boletaceae. **Comments:** The unpleasant taste persists even after cooking. **Similar Species:** Net-like ridges are entirely absent or occur only at the stalk apex in the mild-tasting *T. indecisus* (edible) and the bitter-tasting *T. rubrobrunneus* (edibility unknown). King Bolete (*Boletus edulis*; edible, choice) has white to yellow-brown pores and forms an olive brown spore print; its taste is not bitter.

King Bolete, *Boletus edulis* EDIBLE, choice

Cap: 8–25 cm wide; convex to nearly flat with age; smooth, sticky when wet; yellow-brown, reddish brown, or brown. Undersurface composed of many small, white to yellow pores that age to dull brown. Flesh thick, soft, white. **Stalk:** 10–25 cm long, 2–4 cm thick, enlarged near the base or equal in thickness overall; with white, net-like ridges, especially near the apex; white to yellowish brown. **Spore Print:** Olive brown. **Fruiting:** Solitary or in groups on the ground under conifers and hardwoods; summer, fall. **Range:** Widely distributed throughout N. America. **Family:** Boletaceae. **Comments:** Several varieties of this mushroom are known. **Similar Species:** Several edible, closely related species (such as *B. separans*, with its reddish brown cap and narrower spores) have been described; they differ in some combination of color, tree association, and/or anatomy. Bitter Bolete (*Tylopilus felleus*; inedible) has dark brown, net-like ridges on the stalk and a bitter taste; it forms a pinkish spore print.

▲ Violet-Gray Bolete
Tylopilus plumbeoviolaceus

▼ Bitter Bolete
Tylopilus felleus

▼ King Bolete, *Boletus edulis*

BOLETES

Alice Eastwood's Boletus, Boletus pulcherrimus POISONOUS

Cap: 8–20 cm wide; convex, nearly flat with age; smooth to slightly velvety, with short fibrils in older specimens; grayish olive to reddish brown. Undersurface composed of dark pinkish red to dark red to reddish brown pores that turn blue when bruised. Flesh thick, firm, yellow to greenish yellow, quickly turning blue when injured. **Stalk:** 7–16 cm long, 2–5 cm wide at the apex, up to 10 cm wide at the base; club-shaped, occasionally bulbous or equal in thickness overall; reddish orange to yellowish orange, with dark red, net-like ridges; surface turns blue when bruised. **Spore Print:** Brown. **Fruiting:** Solitary or scattered on the ground in mixed woods; fall. **Range:** Along the Pacific Coast. **Family:** Boletaceae. **Comments:** Formerly known as B. eastwoodiae. One of the largest western boletes, it causes mild to severe gastrointestinal distress. **Similar Species:** Satanic Boletus (B. satanas; poisonous) has a very large, abruptly bulbous, pink-tinged stalk base and lacks reddish brown coloration on the cap. Red-footed Bolete (B. erythropus; poisonous) has a yellowish orange, club-shaped stalk without net-like ridges; it lacks fibrils on the cap and has reddish orange to reddish brown pores.

Frost's Bolete, Boletus frostii EDIBLE (caution)

Cap: 5–15 cm wide; convex to nearly flat with age; smooth, sticky when wet, shiny; blood red to cherry red. Undersurface composed of many small pores, red to reddish brown, bruising dark blue, often with yellowish droplets. Flesh yellow, changing rapidly to blue when exposed. **Stalk:** 4–15 cm long, 1–3 cm thick, enlarged below; dry; with a coarse, partially torn network of raised yellowish ridges; dark red, base often yellow; slowly turning dark blue when bruised. **Spore Print:** Olive brown. **Fruiting:** Solitary, scattered, or in groups on the ground near oak; summer, fall. **Range:** Eastern N. America, west to Mich. **Family:** Boletaceae. **Comments:** Caution: some red-pored boletes that bruise blue are known to cause gastric distress. **Similar Species:** Boletus flammans (edibility unknown) is found under conifers; Boletus rubroflammeus (poisonous) occurs under hardwoods. Both have dry, somewhat duller caps and faint ridges on the stalk. Russell's Bolete (Boletellus russelli; edible) and Shaggy-stalked Bolete (Austroboletus betula; edible) both have coarsely shaggy-netted stalks and yellowish to yellow-olive pores; neither turns blue when bruised.

Common Scaber Stalk, Leccinum scabrum EDIBLE (caution)

Cap: 4–10 cm wide; convex, sometimes depressed in the center; smooth; grayish brown to yellowish brown. Undersurface composed of small, white to yellowish brown pores. Flesh thick, soft, white to pale yellow. **Stalk:** 7–12 cm long, 5–15 mm thick, sometimes enlarged toward the base; white to pale yellow, with coarse, dark, granular projections (scabers) overall. **Spore Print:** Olive brown. **Fruiting:** Solitary, scattered, or in groups on the ground near birch trees; summer, fall. **Range:** Widely distributed in N. America. **Family:** Boletaceae. **Comments:** This "species" is a large complex of several similar-appearing species that are currently being studied and are believed to be edible. **Similar Species:** Red-capped Scaber Stalk (L. aurantiacum; edible) has a reddish orange cap and white flesh that slowly bruises red, then grayish or purplish black. Aspen Scaber Stalk (L. insigne; edible) also has a reddish orange cap, but its white flesh immediately bruises grayish brown to purple-brown.

◀ Alice Eastwood's
Boletus
Boletus pulcherrimus

▼ Frost's Bolete, *Boletus frostii*

▼ Common Scaber Stalk
Leccinum scabrum

BOLETES

Powdery Sulphur Bolete, *Pulveroboletus ravenelii*   EDIBLE

Cap: 2–10 cm wide; convex to nearly flat; powdery to sticky; bright yellow except for reddish orange over the center. Undersurface composed of bright yellow to yellowish green pores that bruise greenish blue; covered by a yellow veil. Flesh thick, soft, yellow, changing to yellow-brown when injured. **Stalk:** 3–8 cm long, 5–10 mm thick, equal in thickness overall; bright yellow to yellowish brown; often with an inconspicuous ring. **Spore Print:** Pale brown. **Fruiting:** Scattered or in groups on the ground in mixed woods; summer, fall. **Range:** Eastern N. America; also known from Calif. **Family:** Boletaceae. **Comments:** Young buttons are completely covered by a yellow, powdery to cottony-membranous universal veil. **Similar Species:** Larch Suillus (*Suillus grevillei*; edible) has a slimy, reddish orange cap with a yellow edge (aging to yellow overall), yellow pores, and a cottony ring on the stalk; it grows under larch trees. Dotted-stalk Suillus (*S. granulatus*; edible) has a slimy, yellowish brown to reddish brown cap, pale yellow pores, and brownish dots on the stalk; it grows under pines.

Old Man of the Woods, *Strobilomyces floccopus*   EDIBLE

Cap: 5–15 cm wide: covered with coarse scales that are partially erect to flattened, cottony, and grayish black; cap surface sometimes gray to white between the scales; cap edge ragged, with torn pieces of a partial veil. Undersurface composed of many small pores, white, becoming gray to black with age, bruising reddish orange and then black. Flesh thick, firm, white, bruising reddish orange and then black. **Stalk:** 4–12 cm long, 1–3 cm thick, nearly equal in thickness overall; cottony; gray; sometimes with torn pieces of a cottony, grayish white veil. **Spore Print:** Black. **Fruiting:** Solitary or scattered on the ground in hardwood and mixed forests; summer, fall. **Range:** Eastern N. America, west to Minn., Mo., and Ariz. **Family:** Boletaceae. **Comments:** Not a favorite, as its flavor is poor. **Similar Species:** *S. confusus* (edible) has smaller, erect, more sharply pointed scales; both *S. floccopus* and *S. confusus* are best distinguished by microscopic examination of the spores. *S. dryophilus* (edibility unknown) is paler and occurs in the Southeast under oak.

Fuscoboletinus spectabilis   EDIBLE

Cap: 4–10 cm wide; convex to nearly flat; sticky to slimy; pale to dark red beneath a layer of coarsely cottony to felt-like scales that are pinkish gray to pinkish red. Undersurface composed of wide, angular to radially elongated pores, yellow to yellowish brown, pinkish where bruised; covered when young by a gelatinous, reddish translucent partial veil. Flesh thick, yellow, slowly becoming pinkish to brown with age. **Stalk:** 4–10 cm long, 1–1.5 cm thick; smooth and yellow above, sheathed with pinkish to red fibrils below; interior solid; with a gelatinous, dark red ring. **Spore Print:** Purplish brown. **Fruiting:** Solitary to scattered in soil among mosses under eastern larch; late summer, early fall. **Range:** North-central to northeastern N. America. **Family:** Boletaceae. **Comments:** A beautiful and distinctive species! **Similar Species:** Rosy Larch Bolete (*F. ochraceoroseus*; edible) has dry, pinkish to pale red scales on the cap; it occurs under western larch in the inland Pacific Northwest.

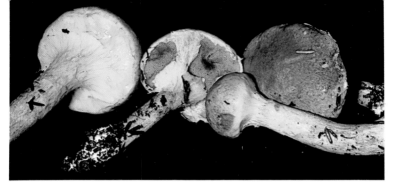

▲ Powdery Sulphur Bolete
Pulveroboletus ravenelii

Old Man of the Woods ▶
Strobilomyces floccopus

▼ *Fuscoboletinus spectabilis*

BOLETES

Painted Suillus, *Suillus pictus*   EDIBLE

Cap: 3–10 cm wide; convex to nearly flat; dry; covered with flat, reddish to reddish brown fibers and scales. Undersurface composed of large yellow pores that bruise yellow-brown; covered by a white partial veil in young specimens. Flesh thick, soft, yellow to pinkish yellow. **Stalk:** 4–10 cm long, 1–2 cm thick, equal in thickness overall or enlarging somewhat near the base; yellowish brown with red and white fibers; interior solid. **Spore Print:** Olive brown. **Fruiting:** Solitary, scattered, or in groups on the ground under eastern white pine; summer, fall. **Range:** Northeastern N. America. **Family:** Boletaceae. **Comments:** In bogs it often fruits in large quantities, even during dry periods. **Similar Species:** Hollow-stalked Larch Suillus (*S. cavipes*; edible) has a scaly, reddish brown cap and stalk and yellow pores; it grows on the ground under larch. Western Painted Suillus (*S. lakei*; edible) has a yellowish cap covered with abundant reddish brown to pinkish scales; it has yellow flesh that turns pink when cut and a yellowish stalk with a white ring; it grows on the ground under Douglas-fir.

Blue-staining Suillus, *Suillus caerulescens*   EDIBLE

Cap: 6–14 cm wide; convex to flat; sticky to slimy; dull reddish to reddish brown near the center, yellowish toward the cap edge; smooth or streaked with small, scattered, cinnamon scales. Undersurface composed of irregularly angular, radially elongated, yellow to yellowish olive pores. Flesh pale yellow. **Stalk:** 2.5–8 cm long, 2–3 cm wide; enlarged and smooth above except for small, net-like ridges at the extreme apex; yellow above and yellow and reddish to dull brown below, turning brown where bruised; with a fibrous, white to dull reddish brown ring; interior solid, yellow, turning blue at the base when exposed. **Spore Print:** Dull cinnamon. **Fruiting:** Solitary, scattered, or in groups in soil under Douglas-fir; fall. **Range:** Pacific Northwest, south into Calif. **Family:** Boletaceae. **Comments:** Often abundant but of low culinary quality. **Similar Species:** Although difficult to distinguish when mature, *S. ponderosus* (edible) has a darker cap and a slimy ring of bright yellow, orange, or reddish brown color.

Slippery Jack, *Suillus luteus*   EDIBLE (caution)

Cap: 5–12 cm wide; convex to nearly flat; smooth, slimy; yellowish brown to reddish brown. Undersurface composed of pale yellow to yellowish olive pores that become brown-dotted with age. Young specimens covered by a white, membranous partial veil, often with lilac tinges below. Flesh thick, soft, white. **Stalk:** 3–8 cm long, 1–2.5 cm thick; yellow near the apex, pale brown with purple streaks below; with a membranous, white (lilac-tinged below) ring. **Spore Print:** Olive brown. **Fruiting:** Solitary, scattered, or in groups on the ground under pine and spruce; late summer, fall. **Range:** Throughout N. America. **Family:** Boletaceae. **Comments:** The slime layer on the cap reportedly can cause diarrhea and should be removed before cooking. **Similar Species:** Slippery Jill (*S. subluteus*; edible after removing the slime layer) has a lighter yellowish brown cap, a thinner stalk, and a baggy, flaring, membranous ring without lilac coloration. *S. decipiens* (edible) has a yellowish orange to reddish orange cap covered by dry, yellowish brown fibers and scales; it has yellow pores, a white to pinkish partial veil in young specimens, and a pinkish cinnamon stalk.

▲ Painted Suillus, *Suillus pictus*

▲ Blue-staining Suillus
Suillus caerulescens

▼ Slippery Jack
Suillus luteus

CHANTERELLES AND SIMILAR FUNGI

Nivatogastrium nubigenum   EDIBILITY UNKNOWN

Cap: 1–6 cm wide; ovoid to somewhat irregular, center often flat, wrinkled where attached to the stalk; smooth, sticky when wet; yellowish tan to white. Flesh thin, watery-white to cream; odor *very* sweet. **Gills:** Seen well only if cut open; attached to the stalk, irregularly arranged and contorted, fused to one another at numerous points; dull cinnamon brown. **Stalk:** 5–25 mm long, 5–12 mm thick, equal in thickness overall or enlarged below; smooth or with flat, matted fibrils; white; interior solid, white, rusty brown near the base; with a fibrous, white veil that forms a disappearing, fibrous ring *if* the cap expands. **Spore Color:** Pale brown. **Fruiting:** Solitary, scattered, or in small clusters on conifer wood and woody debris near melting snow; late spring, early summer. **Range:** Alpine areas of western N. America. **Family:** Cortinariaceae. **Comments:** A characteristic element of the western snowbank mushroom flora. The cap rarely unfolds and does not make a spore print. **Similar Species:** *Endoptychum agaricoides* (edibility unknown) has a nearly round to cone-shaped, white to dull brown cap and a short white stalk; it fruits in soil in summer and fall and is widely distributed throughout N. America.

Lobster Fungus, *Hypomyces lactifluorum*   EDIBLE (caution)

Fruiting Body: A bright orange to reddish orange layer with numerous very small, partially embedded, pimple-like bumps (like sandpaper to the touch) growing on and covering the cap, stalk, and gills of several species of the mushroom genera *Lactarius* and *Russula*. **Stalk:** Absent (except on host mushroom). **Fruiting:** Solitary or scattered on the ground under conifers and hardwoods; summer, fall. **Range:** Widely distributed in N. America. **Family:** Hypocreaceae. **Comments:** This species is edible if found on an edible mushroom host. Because edibility is determined by the mushroom on which the *Hypomyces* is growing, caution is advised. **Similar Species:** *H. luteovirens* (edibility unknown) also grows on *Lactarius* and *Russula* species but is yellow-green in color. Golden Hypomyces (*H. chrysospermus;* inedible) is found on boletes. Amanita Mold (*H. hyalinus*) attacks several species of *Amanita,* changing them into thick, club-shaped, whitish structures; its edibility depends on the edibility of the host mushroom—a positive identification of the host *Amanita* is necessary.

Black Trumpet, *Craterellus fallax*   EDIBLE, choice

Fruiting Body: 1–6 cm wide, 4–12 cm tall; funnel-shaped and hollow. Inner surface scaly, grayish black to brownish black. Outer surface (undersurface) smooth or nearly so, grayish brown to orange-brown. Flesh thin, fibrous, grayish brown; odor and taste fruity. **Stalk:** Indistinct—a short extension of the fruiting body; brownish black. **Spore Print:** Pale yellowish salmon. **Fruiting:** Solitary, scattered, or in groups on the ground in hardwood forests; summer, fall. **Range:** Throughout N. America. **Family:** Cantharellaceae. **Comments:** Because of its color, it is well hidden by leaves and easily passed over. **Similar Species:** Horn of Plenty (*C. cornucopioides;* edible, choice) is dark grayish brown and forms a white spore print. Fragrant Chanterelle (*C. odoratus;* edible) develops a cluster of funnel-shaped, bright orange fruiting bodies with a fragrant odor; it occurs in the Southeast.

▲ *Nivatogastrium nubigenum*

▲ Lobster Fungus
Hypomyces lactifluorum

Black Trumpet ▶
Craterellus fallax

CHANTERELLES AND SIMILAR FUNGI

Smooth Chanterelle, *Cantharellus lateritius*   EDIBLE

Cap: 2.5–9 cm wide, flat, often slightly depressed in the center to somewhat funnel-shaped; cap edge decurved, becoming wavy; surface smooth or with fine scales; orange to yellowish orange to orange-yellow, fading with age. Undersurface orange-yellow (paler than the cap), smooth or with very shallow, thick, blunt, irregular, wrinkle-like folds running down the stalk. Flesh thin except at the center, white to cream, tinted with the cap color near the surface; odor often fruity. **Stalk:** 1.7–4.5 cm long, 1–1.6 cm thick, tapering toward the base; smooth; dark to pale orange-yellow; interior solid, white. **Spore Print:** Light yellow-orange. **Fruiting:** Solitary, scattered, or in small groups in soil under hardwoods; summer, early fall. **Range:** Eastern N. America, more common in the central and southern regions. **Family:** Cantharellaceae. **Comments:** Formerly known as *Craterellus cantharellus.* **Similar Species:** The ubiquitous Chanterelle (*Cantharellus cibarius;* edible, choice) is also orange to orange-yellow; its gill-like folds are more regular and well-developed, and it has a single, solid stalk. Fragrant Chanterelle (*Craterellus odoratus;* edible) has an orange to orange-yellow coloration and exhibits clusters of hollow, stalked caps fused on a common base; it occurs in the Southeast.

Scaly Vase Chanterelle, *Gomphus floccosus*   INEDIBLE

Fruiting Body: 5–12 cm wide near the top, 6–18 cm tall; funnel-shaped, with coarse scales. Inner surface yellow-orange to orange-brown. Outer surface (undersurface) wrinkled to vein-like, dull cream or dull pale yellow to yellow-brown. Flesh thick, firm, white. **Stalk:** An extension of the fruiting body; tapering downward, colored like the cap; interior hollow. **Spore Print:** Brownish yellow. **Fruiting:** Solitary or in groups under conifers or in mixed woods; summer, fall. **Range:** Throughout N. America. **Family:** Cantharellaceae. **Comments:** This species is listed as edible in some books but is unpalatable; it has been reported to cause gastric distress. **Similar Species:** Kauffman's Gomphus (*Gomphus kauffmanii;* inedible) has very large, coarse scales and occurs in the West. Pig's Ear Gomphus (*G. clavatus;* edible, choice) is purplish to yellow-brown with a purplish to purple-brown undersurface; it occurs in overlapping clusters.

Craterellus caeruleofuscus   EDIBILITY UNKNOWN

Cap: 1.5–7 cm wide; trumpet-shaped to vase-shaped; edge decurved when young, becoming wavy with age; smooth to wrinkled; dark brown, fading to grayish-brown. Undersurface wrinkled; with forked, blunt-edged veins descending the stalk; dark gray, fading with age to pale grayish brown. Flesh thin, membranous, grayish; odor not distinct. **Stalk:** 2.5–5 cm long, 4–13 mm thick; equal in thickness overall or narrowed somewhat toward the base; grayish brown; interior hollow. **Spore Print:** White. **Fruiting:** Scattered, in groups, or in clusters on the ground among mosses, usually in conifer woods; summer, fall. **Range:** Northeastern N. America, west to Mich. **Family:** Cantharellaceae. **Comments:** This mushroom prefers cool, shady areas and fruits abundantly in mossy woods after rainy periods. **Similar Species:** *C. cinereus* (edibility unknown) forms blackish brown caps with raised, forked, thickened, brownish gray veins; it lacks a distinct odor. *C. foetidus* (edibility unknown) has a grayish brown cap and a very fragrant, sickeningly sweet odor; it grows in mixed woods.

▲ Smooth Chanterelle
Cantharellus lateritius

▲ Scaly Vase Chanterelle
Gomphus floccosus

▼ *Craterellus caeruleofuscus*

CHANTERELLES AND SIMILAR FUNGI

Chanterelle, *Cantharellus cibarius*   EDIBLE, choice

Cap: 2.5–13 cm wide; convex to nearly flat with age; smooth; yellow to yellowish orange. Undersurface composed of thick, forked, blunt, vein-like to gill-like ridges interconnected by crossveins and extending down the stalk; yellow to yellowish orange. Flesh firm, thick, pale yellow; odor sweet, fruit-like; taste mild to somewhat spicy. **Stalk:** 2.5–10 cm long, 1–2 cm thick; narrowing somewhat at the base; pale yellow to yellowish orange. **Spore Print:** Pale yellow. **Fruiting:** Solitary or in groups on the ground under conifers or hardwoods; summer to fall (late fall in Calif.) **Range:** Throughout N. America. **Family:** Cantharellaceae. **Comments:** A choice specimen for the table, but be careful not to confuse it with the poisonous Jack O'Lanterns. **Similar Species:** The orange Jack O'Lantern of the East (*Omphalotus olearius*; poisonous) and the olive-tinted orange-yellow Western Jack O'Lantern (*O. olivascens*; poisonous) occur in fused clusters on hardwood stumps and buried wood in lawns and have sharp, knife blade-like gills. Compared with *Cantharellus cibarius,* White Chanterelle (*C. subalbidus*; edible, choice) is similar in stature but has a white to pale coloration; it forms a white spore print. Smooth Chanterelle (*C. lateritius*; edible) of northeastern N. America is also similar, but the lower cap surface is nearly smooth. Cinnabar Red Chanterelle (*C. cinnabarinus*; edible) is smaller and has a reddish orange cap and pinkish red, gill-like ridges on the cap undersurface.

Trumpet Chanterelle, *Cantharellus tubaeformis*   EDIBLE, choice

Cap: 1–7 cm wide; convex to nearly flat or depressed with age; wrinkled to somewhat scaly; edge inrolled, becoming wavy; yellow-brown to dark brown. Undersurface composed of widely spaced, forked, blunt, gill-like ridges with crossveins, descending the stalk; yellowish brown to grayish purple. Flesh thin, firm, grayish to yellowish brown. **Stalk:** 2–5 cm long, 4–10 mm thick; nearly equal in thickness overall; smooth; yellow-orange; interior becoming hollow with age. **Spore Print:** Pale yellow. **Fruiting:** In groups in wet, mossy ground or in sphagnum moss in bogs; summer, fall. **Range:** Throughout northern N. America. **Family:** Cantharellaceae. **Similar Species:** Yellow-footed Chanterelle (*C. xanthopus*; edible) has an orange-brown cap with a smooth to slightly wrinkled, yellow-brown undersurface. Flame-colored Chanterelle (*C. ignicolor*; edibility unknown) has a small, yellowish orange cap and a blunt-edged, forked, yellow-orange to yellowish brown undersurface.

Clustered Blue Chanterelle, *Polyozellus multiplex*   EDIBLE

Fruiting Body: 2–10 cm wide, 6–15 cm tall; composed of clusters of vase-shaped to fan-shaped, depressed caps with wavy edges; grayish purple or bluish gray to dark gray, becoming blackish with age. Undersurface composed of vein-like folds that descend the stalk, grayish purple. Flesh thick, soft, grayish purple; odor aromatic. **Stalk:** 2–5 cm long, 1–2.5 cm thick; grayish purple, aging to black; mostly fused with other stalks near the point of attachment. **Spore Print:** White. **Fruiting:** Clustered on the ground in conifer woods; summer, fall. **Range:** Throughout northern N. America. **Family:** Cantharellaceae. **Comments:** This mushroom may be found in dense clusters sometimes over a foot in diameter. **Similar Species:** Fragrant Chanterelle (*Craterellus odoratus*; edible; *see photo*), which also occurs in clusters, is orange to orange-yellow; it occurs in the Southeast.

Chanterelle ▶
Cantharellus cibarius

▼ Trumpet Chanterelle
Cantharellus tubaeformis

▼ Clustered Blue Chanterelle
Polyozellus multiplex

▼ Fragrant Chanterelle
Craterellus odoratus

STALKLESS AND LATERAL-STALKED FUNGI

Common Split Gill, *Schizophyllum commune*   INEDIBLE

Cap: 1–3 cm wide; fan-shaped, convex to nearly flat; densely hairy; white to grayish white. Undersurface with widely spaced, elongated, gill-like folds that are split on their free edge; white to pinkish gray. Flesh thin, leathery and flexible, white. **Stalk:** Absent. **Spore Print:** White. **Fruiting:** Solitary, scattered, or often in overlapping clusters on dead branches, logs, and stumps of hardwood trees; year-round. **Range:** Throughout N. America. **Family:** Schizophyllaceae. **Comments:** Commonly encountered and easily recognized by the hairy cap and split gills. Too small and tough to be eaten. **Similar Species:** Crimped Gill (*Plicaturopsis crispa;* inedible) is yellowish brown and stalkless; it has crimped, shallow, gill-like folds and occurs in cooler parts of eastern N. America.

Evasive Agaric, *Crepidotus versutus*   EDIBILITY UNKNOWN

Cap: 5–15 mm wide; fan-shaped to kidney-shaped, with an incurved and often wavy edge; velvety to hairy; white. Flesh thin, soft, white. **Gills:** Radiating from the point of attachment, somewhat separated; white when young, becoming dull rusty brown; edges smooth to delicately toothed. **Stalk:** Absent. **Spore Print:** Cinnamon brown. **Fruiting:** Solitary or in overlapping clusters on the bark of hardwoods; summer, fall. **Range:** Eastern N. America. **Family:** Crepidotaceae. **Comments:** *Crepidotus* is a large genus with more than 100 species. Little is known about their edibility, perhaps because of their small size. **Similar Species:** Flat Crep (*C. applanatus;* edibility unknown) is larger; it has a smooth to slightly hairy, shell-shaped, white cap with closely spaced gills; conspicuous white threads are present at the point of attachment.

Multicolor Gill Polypore, *Lenzites betulina*   INEDIBLE

Cap: 2–10 cm wide; slightly convex to nearly flat, fan-shaped to semicircular; hairy; ranges from white to green, grayish brown, or reddish brown; sometimes with several multicolored zones. Undersurface composed of radially elongated pores (usually appearing gill-like) that are tough and dull white to brownish. Flesh thick, fibrous, white. **Stalk:** Absent. **Spore Print:** White. **Fruiting:** Solitary, scattered, or in overlapping clusters on wood; year-round. **Range:** Widely distributed in N. America. **Family:** Polyporaceae. **Comments:** The cap may be covered by algae, which gives it a bright green color. **Similar Species:** Yellow-Red Gill Polypore (*Gloeophyllum sepiarium;* inedible) forms semicircular, hairy, yellowish red caps with yellow-brown, gill-like pores. Thin-maze Flat Polypore (*Daedaleopsis confragosa;* inedible) has a stalkless, grayish brown, zoned cap and elongated, maze-like pores. Mossy Maze Polypore (*Cerrena unicolor;* inedible) has a stalkless, often algae-covered, white to grayish or green cap; its elongated, grayish pores are maze-like or tooth-like.

▲ Common Split Gill, *Schizophyllum commune*

▲ Evasive agaric
Crepidotus versutus

Multicolor Gill
Polypore ▶
Lenzites betulina

STALKLESS AND LATERAL-STALKED FUNGI

Bear Lentinus, *Lentinellus ursinus*   EDIBILITY UNKNOWN

Cap: 2–10 cm wide; fan-shaped, convex to nearly flat with age; with thick, dark brown hairs, especially near the base; cinnamon brown to reddish brown. Flesh firm, white to pinkish brown; odor fruity; taste bitter. **Gills:** Closely spaced; edges sawtooth-like to irregularly torn; off white to pinkish brown. **Stalk:** Absent. **Spore Print:** White. **Fruiting:** Solitary, scattered, or in groups and overlapping clusters on conifer and hardwood logs; summer, fall. **Range:** Widely distributed in N. America. **Family:** Tricholomataceae. **Comments:** Viewed from above, the hairy cap may sometimes resemble a bear's paw. **Similar Species:** *L. vulpinus* (edibility unknown) is similar in color, shape, and gill spacing but has a rough, radially grooved cap and white hairs. *L. montanus* (edibility unknown) fruits on wood at high elevations in western mountains during spring and early summer; it has widely spaced gills. *L. cochleatus* (edibility unknown) has a vase-shaped cap and a distinct stalk; it grows on decaying stumps and buried wood.

Orange Mock Oyster, *Phyllotopsis nidulans*   INEDIBLE

Cap: 2–8 cm wide; fan-shaped, broadly convex to nearly flat; yellowish orange to orange; covered with a dense layer of short hairs; dry; edge inrolled in young specimens. Flesh thick, firm, pale orange-brown; odor and taste disagreeable. **Gills:** Attached to a hairy base, closely spaced; yellowish orange to orange-brown. **Stalk:** Absent or nearly so. **Spore Print:** Pale pink. **Fruiting:** Scattered or in overlapping clusters on decaying conifer and hardwood trees, stumps, and logs; summer, fall (and winter in the South). **Range:** Widely distributed in N. America. **Family:** Tricholomataceae. **Comments:** Inedible because of its disagreeable odor and taste. **Similar Species:** Ruddy Panus (*Panus rudis*; inedible) has a densely hairy, reddish brown (aging to pinkish tan) cap; it forms a white spore print. Late Fall Oyster (*Panellus serotinus*; edible) exhibits a yellowish green cap and yellowish gills.

Netted Rhodotus, *Rhodotus palmatus*   EDIBILITY UNKNOWN

Cap: 2–8 cm wide, broadly convex; edge incurved in young specimens. Surface composed of net-like ridges and pits; reddish pink to a pinkish flesh color, fading to pale orange-yellow. Flesh thick, rubbery, with a pinkish flesh color. **Gills:** Attached to the stalk, closely spaced; interconnected by fine veins; pink to pale salmon. **Stalk:** 2.5–5 cm long, 3–6 mm thick; off-center, curved, enlarged below; smooth; light pink. **Spore Print:** Pink. **Fruiting:** Solitary to scattered on old hardwood logs; summer, fall. **Range:** Eastern N. America. **Family:** Tricholomataceae. **Comments:** Although not common, this species is easily recognized by the combination of net-like ridges on the cap surface, lateral stalk, and pinkish coloration. **Similar Species:** Orange Mock Oyster (*Phyllotopsis nidulans*; inedible) is similar in size but exhibits an unpleasant odor and taste; it has a hairy cap without ridges, is more orange in coloration, and lacks a distinct stalk.

▲ Bear Lentinus
Lentinellus ursinus

▼ Orange Mock Oyster
Phyllotopsis nidulans

▼ Netted Rhodotus
Rhodotus palmatus

STALKLESS AND LATERAL-STALKED FUNGI

Luminescent Panellus, *Panellus stipticus*   EDIBLE

Cap: 1–4 cm wide; shell-shaped to kidney-shaped; dry, minutely hairy, with very small, scurfy scales when the cap expands; tan to yellowish brown. Flesh thin, tough, pallid. **Gills:** Descending down the stalk, closely spaced; pale cinnamon. **Stalk:** 2–20 mm long, 2–3 mm thick; off-center (attached at or near the cap side), tapered toward the base; minutely hairy; pallid to pale tan. **Spore Print:** White. **Fruiting:** Scattered or in groups in large numbers on hardwood logs and stumps; spring, summer, fall. **Range:** Throughout N. America. **Family:** Tricholomataceae. **Comments:** The bioluminescent gills glow yellowish green in the dark, making this species one of the "ghosts of the forest." **Similar Species:** Ruddy Panus (*Panus rudis,* inedible) is larger, has a reddish brown cap that fades to pinkish tan, and exhibits lilac tinges when young, fresh, and moist.

Late Fall Oyster, *Panellus serotinus*   EDIBLE

Cap: 2.5–10 cm wide; fan-shaped to shell-shaped; smooth, slimy when wet; yellowish green to olive green. Flesh thick, firm, white; taste bitter. **Gills:** Attached to the stalk, somewhat separated; yellow to pale orange. **Stalk:** 1–2 cm long, 5–15 mm thick; off-center; yellow to yellowish brown. **Spore Print:** Pale yellow. **Fruiting:** Solitary, scattered, or in overlapping clusters on conifer and hardwood logs; fall, early winter. **Range:** Widely distributed in N. America. **Family:** Tricholomataceae. **Comments:** Also called Greenback. Although edible, this species may have to be boiled to remove the bitter taste. **Similar Species:** Ruddy Panus (*Panus rudis;* inedible) has a hairy, reddish brown to tan cap. Orange Mock Oyster (*Phyllotopsis nidulans;* inedible) has a hairy, orange cap and a disagreeable odor. Luminescent Panellus (*Panellus stipticus;* edible) is characterized by smaller, hairy, yellowish brown caps and the production by the gills of a yellowish green light in the dark.

Oyster Mushroom, *Pleurotus ostreatus*   EDIBLE, choice

Cap: 5–20 cm wide; broadly convex to nearly flat, shaped like an oyster shell; smooth, slippery when wet; white to grayish brown. Flesh thick, firm, white; odor of fruit or licorice. **Gills:** Descending the stalk, closely spaced; white. **Stalk:** 1–2.5 cm long, 1–2 cm thick; off-center; white; absent in some specimens. **Spore Print:** White to pale lilac. **Fruiting:** Solitary or, more often, in overlapping clusters on decaying hardwood trees (especially poplar, willow, and beech), logs, and stumps; spring, fall. **Range:** Throughout N. America. **Family:** Tricholomataceae. **Comments:** Some authors recognize lilac-spored specimens as *P. sapidus* and white-spored specimens as *P. ostreatus.* This mushroom may represent a complex of several very similar species. **Similar Species:** Angel's Wings (*Pleurocybella porrigens;* edible) has smaller, stalkless, white caps and thinner flesh; it grows scattered or in clusters on wood. Veiled Oyster (*Pleurotus dryinus;* edible) has a cottony, white cap with torn veil fragments on the edge and a well-developed stalk with a delicate ring. Elm Oyster (*Hypsizygus tessulatus;* edible) has a cracked, white to tan cap with an off-center stalk; it grows on decaying hardwoods.

▲ Luminescent Panellus
Panellus stipticus

▼ Late Fall Oyster
Panellus serotinus

▼ Oyster Mushroom
Pleurotus ostreatus

MUSHROOMS WITH RING AND CUP

Destroying Angel, *Amanita virosa*   DEADLY

Cap: 5–12 cm wide; convex to nearly flat with age; smooth, lacking warts, slightly sticky when fresh; white. Flesh thick, firm, white. **Gills:** Free of the stalk or nearly so, closely spaced; white. **Stalk:** 7–20 cm long, 5–20 mm thick, enlarging somewhat toward the base; cottony; white; covered at the base by a membranous, sac-like, white cup and near the apex by a membranous, white ring. **Spore Print:** White. **Fruiting:** Solitary, scattered, or in groups on the ground near conifers or hardwoods; summer, fall. **Range:** Throughout N. America. **Family:** Amanitaceae. **Comments:** Be certain not to confuse young *Amanita* buttons with puffballs. **Similar Species:** The following *Amanita* species are nearly identical and are best distinguished with a microscope: *A. bisporigera* (deadly) is smaller and has a more slender stalk; *A. verna* (deadly) has a smoother stalk.

Death Cap, *Amanita phalloides*   DEADLY

Cap: 7–15 cm wide; convex to nearly flat; smooth, somewhat sticky when wet; yellowish green to yellowish brown, with darker, finer, flattened hairs near the center. Flesh thin, firm, white; odor somewhat disagreeable. **Gills:** Free of the stalk or nearly so, closely spaced; white. **Stalk:** 7–12 cm long, 1.5–2 cm thick; white; enlarging downward to a basal bulb within a white, sac-like cup; bearing a fragile, white ring. **Spore Print:** White. **Fruiting:** Solitary or in groups on the ground in conifer and hardwood forests; fall, early winter. **Range:** Eastern N. America, west to Ohio, Pacific Coast; apparently spreading. **Family:** Amanitaceae. **Comments:** This deadly mushroom contains potent amatoxins, which affect kidney and liver function. The onset of symptoms is often delayed for 10 or more hours. **Similar Species:** Destroying Angel (*A. virosa*; deadly) and some other deadly *Amanita* species are pure white and lack a disagreeable odor.

Coccora, *Amanita calyptrata*   EDIBLE (caution)

Cap: 7–35 cm wide; nearly egg-shaped when young, becoming convex to nearly flat with age; smooth, with short grooves at the cap edge, sticky when wet; rich yellow-brown, darker brown in the center, usually with a large, thick, irregular, white surface patch. Flesh very thick, solid, white. **Gills:** Free of the stalk or nearly so, closely spaced; white to very pale yellow. **Stalk:** 10–25 cm long, 2–3 cm thick, equal in thickness overall; smooth; white to cream yellow; interior stuffed to hollow; with a large, thick, sac-like cup at the base. Ring is flaring, membranous, thin, and fragile; white to cream yellow. **Spore Print:** White. **Fruiting:** Solitary, scattered, or in clusters in mixed woods; fall. **Range:** Pacific Coast (into Canada). **Family:** Amanitaceae. **Comments:** The entire fruiting body is covered with a thick, white, tissue layer (universal veil) in the button stage (*see photo*). Because of possible confusion with other *Amanita* species, exercise caution if collecting one, especially the buttons, for the table. **Similar Species:** A form of Caesar's Amanita (*A. caesarea*; edible) found in Ariz., N.M., and Europe, is similar, but it has a reddish orange cap and yellow gills.

Destroying Angel ▶
Amanita virosa

▼ Death Cap
Amanita phalloides

▼ Coccora
Amanita calyptrata

▼ Coccora (button stage)
Amanita calyptrata

MUSHROOMS WITH RING AND CUP

American Caesar's Mushroom, *Amanita hemibapha*
EDIBLE (caution)

Cap: 5–12 cm wide; convex to nearly flat with age; usually with a knob in the center; sticky; reddish orange or yellowish orange; with shallow grooves near the edge. Flesh thin, soft, pale yellow or white. **Gills:** Free of the stalk or nearly so, closely spaced; yellow; covered by a yellow partial veil in young specimens. **Stalk:** 7–15 cm long, 5–20 mm thick; yellow, sometimes with yellow-orange scales; with a yellow, membrane-like ring and a white, sac-like cup at the base. **Spore Print:** White. **Fruiting:** Solitary or in groups on the ground in mixed woods; summer, fall. **Range:** Throughout eastern N. America. **Family:** Amanitaceae. **Comments:** Also known as *A. umbonata, A. jacksonii,* and *A. caesarea;* the nomenclature of this species is currently under study. Be certain that a specimen is not *A. muscaria.* The white sac-like cup is distinctive. **Similar Species:** False Caesar's Mushroom (*A. parcivolvata;* edibility unknown) has a red to orange-yellow cap and yellow patches; it has no ring or sac-like cup.

Citron Amanita, *Amanita citrina*   EDIBILITY UNKNOWN

Cap: 4–10 cm wide; convex to nearly flat with age; greenish yellow to yellowish brown, aging to pale yellow near the edge; often covered with pale yellow or white patches. Flesh soft, thick, white. **Gills:** Free of the stalk or nearly so, closely spaced; white; covered by a yellowish white partial veil in young specimens. **Stalk:** 8–10 cm long, 8–15 mm thick; enlarging downward to a soft basal bulb with a narrow collar; white; with a white or yellowish white ring. **Spore Print:** White. **Fruiting:** Solitary or in groups on the ground in mixed woods; summer, fall. **Range:** Throughout eastern N. America. **Family:** Amanitaceae. **Comments:** The gills have a bleach-like odor. **Similar Species:** Purple-Brown Amanita (*A. porphyria;* edibility unknown) has a brown cap, a gray ring on the stalk, and an abruptly bulbous base.

Blusher, *Amanita rubescens*   EDIBLE (caution)

Cap: 5–15 cm wide; convex to nearly flat with age, sometimes with a low knob; somewhat sticky; reddish brown mixed with pale cream; developing reddish to dull wine red discolorations with age; covered with irregular warts that are olive gray, pinkish white, or white. Flesh thick, soft, white, staining reddish when injured. **Gills:** Free of the stalk or nearly so, closely spaced; white or pale yellowish white, developing reddish or pinkish brown discolorations over time; covered by a white partial veil in young specimens. **Stalk:** 8–20 cm long, 5–20 mm thick, enlarging downward to a bulbous base; white, often streaked with pinkish red and developing reddish discolorations; with a white to pink ring and scattered white to pink patches on the stalk base. **Spore Print:** White. **Fruiting:** Solitary or in groups on the ground under conifers and hardwoods; summer, fall (year-round in Calif.). **Range:** Eastern N. America; Calif. **Family:** Amanitaceae. **Comments:** The combination of reddish brown cap, development of reddish discolorations, and grayish white to whitish warts is characteristic of this species. **Similar Species:** Cleft-foot Amanita (*A. brunnescens;* edibility not clearly established; *see photo*) has a brownish cap and a vertically split basal bulb; it bruises reddish brown.

▲ American Caesar's Mushroom
Amanita hemibapha

▲ Citron Amanita
Amanita citrina

▲ Blusher
Amanita rubescens

▲ Cleft-foot Amanita
Amanita brunnescens

MUSHROOMS WITH RING AND CUP

Gemmed Amanita, *Amanita gemmata*   EDIBILITY UNKNOWN

Cap: 3–10 cm wide; convex to nearly flat with age, sometimes slightly depressed in the center; smooth, sticky; pale yellow to pinkish yellow; with white, wart-like patches and shallow grooves near the edge. Flesh thin, soft, white. **Gills:** Free of the stalk or nearly so, closely spaced; white; covered by a white partial veil in young specimens. **Stalk:** 5–12 cm long, 5–20 mm thick; equal in thickness overall or enlarging somewhat into a small, rounded, white basal bulb with a narrow collar; white; with a white ring. **Spore Print:** White. **Fruiting:** Solitary or in groups on the ground in conifer and hardwood forests or in grassy areas near pines; summer, fall. **Range:** Throughout N. America. **Family:** Amanitaceae. **Comments:** The white, wart-like patches are easily washed off by rain. **Similar Species:** Panther (*A. pantherina;* poisonous) has a light brown cap, white warts, and a basal bulb with a collar; it is found under Douglas-fir.

Fly Agaric, *Amanita muscaria*   POISONOUS

Cap: 5–26 cm wide; convex to flat; moist and slightly sticky; yellow-orange or red, with white patches. Flesh firm, white. **Gills:** Free of the stalk or nearly so, closely spaced; white. **Stalk:** 5–15 cm long, 1–3 cm thick, enlarging somewhat at the base; white; with 2 or 3 concentric bands of cottony tissue near the base and a fragile, membranous ring near the apex. **Spore Print:** White. **Fruiting:** Solitary or in groups on the ground in conifer and mixed forests; summer, fall (and early winter in coastal Calif.). **Range:** Throughout N. America. **Family:** Amanitaceae. **Comments:** Specimens with red caps are most common in the West; those with yellow-orange caps (*see photo opposite*) are most common in the East. There is also an all-white variety. This mushroom causes delirium and copious sweating. **Similar Species:** Yellow Patches (*A. flavoconia;* edibility unknown) is smaller and has yellow patches on the cap.

Yellow Patches, *Amanita flavoconia*   EDIBILITY UNKNOWN

Cap: 3–7 cm wide; convex to nearly flat; sticky; bright yellow to yellowish orange; covered with yellow, wart-like patches. Flesh thin, soft, pale yellow. **Gills:** Free of the stalk or nearly so, closely spaced; white; covered by a white to pale yellow partial veil in young specimens. **Stalk:** 5–10 cm long, 5–15 mm thick, enlarging toward the base to an oval basal bulb that is covered with scattered, yellow, wart-like patches; white to pale yellow; with a white to yellow ring. **Spore Print:** White. **Fruiting:** Solitary or in groups on the ground in hardwood and mixed forests; summer, fall. **Range:** Throughout eastern N. America. **Family:** Amanitaceae. **Comments:** The combination of a bright yellow cap with yellow patches and the absence of any red discolorations is characteristic. **Similar Species:** Yellow Blusher (*A. flavorubescens;* edibility unknown; *see photo*) has dull reddish discolorations near the stalk base—on the surface or (more often) in the flesh. *A. frostiana* (edibility unknown) has a collar-like cup, white warts on the cap surface, and grooves on the cap edge; unlike *A. flavoconia* and *A. flavorubescens,* its spores do not change color in iodine.

▲ Gemmed Amanita, *Amanita gemmata*

▲ Fly Agaric, *Amanita muscaria*

▲ Yellow Patches
Amanita flavoconia

▲ Yellow Blusher
Amanita flavorubescens

MUSHROOMS WITH CUP ONLY

Grisette, *Amanita vaginata*　EDIBLE (caution)

Cap: 5–10 cm wide; oval, becoming convex to nearly flat with age; with a central knob and grooves near the edge; smooth; white or gray to yellowish gray; sometimes with white patches. Flesh thin, soft, white. **Gills:** Free of the stalk or nearly so, closely spaced; white. **Stalk:** 10–20 cm long, 1–1.5 cm thick, sometimes widening toward the base; white; with a white cup. **Spore Print:** White. **Fruiting:** Solitary or in groups on the ground in woods among mosses or on lawns near trees; summer, fall (also winter in Calif.). **Range:** Throughout N. America. **Family:** Amanitaceae. **Comments:** Also known as *Amanitopsis vaginata.* Unlike most other *Amanita* species, this lacks a prominent ring. **Similar Species:** Tawny Grisette (*Amanita fulva*; edible) has a reddish brown or tan cap, small grooves along the edge, and a white stalk and cup. Strangulated Amanita (*Amanita ceciliae,* formerly *A. inaurata*; edibility unknown) has a dark grayish brown or brownish black cap with grooves near the edge, grayish patches on the cap, and grayish tissue forming a cup at the base of the stalk.

Smooth Volvariella, *Volvariella speciosa*　EDIBLE

Cap: 5–15 cm wide; convex to nearly flat with age; sticky, becoming dry and shiny; grayish white. Flesh thick, firm, white. **Gills:** Free of the stalk, crowded together; white, becoming pink with age. **Stalk:** 8–20 cm long, 5–20 mm thick; dry, smooth; white; with a deep, white, sac-like cup at the base. **Spore Print:** Pink to brownish pink. **Fruiting:** Solitary, scattered, or in large groups on the ground in open places and woods; summer, fall (fall and winter in Calif.). **Range:** Widely distributed in N. America; most common on the West Coast. **Family:** Pluteaceae. **Comments:** This mushroom often fruits in very large numbers in cultivated fields, along highways, and in similar habitats. Although it is edible, most people find it rather bland. Because fungi may accumulate toxic heavy metals, we do not recommend eating any mushroom growing along or near roadsides. **Similar Species:** Parasitic Volvariella (*V. surrecta*; edibility unknown) has a smaller white cap and grows on the caps of Cloudy Clitocybe (*Clitocybe nebularis*; inedible).

Tree Volvariella, *Volvariella bombycina*　EDIBLE

Cap: 5–20 cm wide; oval, becoming convex to flat with age; silky, with fine hairs, dry; white to pale yellowish white. Flesh thin, soft, white. **Gills:** Free of the stalk, very closely spaced; white when young, aging to pink. **Stalk:** 6–20 cm long, 1–2 cm thick, widening at the base; dry; white; surrounded at the base by a deep, white, sac-like cup. **Spore Print:** Pink to pinkish brown. **Fruiting:** Solitary or in groups on hardwood trees, stumps, and logs; summer, fall. **Range:** Throughout eastern N. America. **Family:** Pluteaceae. **Comments:** The combination of silky white cap, white stalk, pink gills, and pink spore print is characteristic. **Similar Species:** All *Pluteus* species also form pink to pinkish brown spore prints but lack a cup. *Amanita* species grow on the ground and form white spore prints. *Volvariella pusilla* (edibility unknown) has a tiny white cap (5–30 mm wide) with silky fibers and short lines visible at the cap edge when moist; it grows in soil in gardens and greenhouses and on lawns. *V. hypopithys* (edibility unknown) has a medium-size white cap (2–5 cm wide) with silky to scaly fibers and lacks the short lines at the cap edge when moist; it grows on the ground in woods.

▲ Grisette, *Amanita vaginata*

▲ Smooth Volvariella, *Volvariella speciosa*

Tree Volvariella ▶
Volvariella bombycina

MUSHROOMS WITH RING ONLY

RING MEMBRANOUS OR COTTONY

White Matsutake, *Tricholoma magnivelare*   EDIBLE, choice
Cap: 5–18 cm wide; convex to nearly flat with age; cap edge cottony and inrolled when young; smooth when very young, usually soon becoming scaly; dry to sticky (when wet); white, becoming reddish brown to yellowish brown with age. Flesh thick, firm, white; odor fragrant. **Gills:** Attached to the stalk, closely spaced; white, bruising brownish. **Stalk:** 5–15 cm long, 2–4 cm thick, typically tapering toward the base; white, covered by patches of brownish tissue below a white cottony ring. **Spore Print:** White. **Fruiting:** Scattered or in groups in sandy or wet soil under conifers, especially hemlock and fir; fall, winter. **Range:** Widely distributed in northern N. America. **Family:** Tricholomataceae. **Comments:** Formerly known as *Armillaria ponderosa.* **Similar Species:** Swollen-stalked Cat (*Catathelasma ventricosa*; edible) has a double ring and lacks a fragrant odor. Fragrant Armillaria (*Armillaria caligata*; edible) has a smaller, dark cinnamon brown cap, a strong spicy odor, and a white ring with cinnamon brown patches below. Fetid Armillaria (*A. zelleri*; edible) has a scaly, orange-brown cap and a white ring with orange-brown scales below; it exhibits a disagreeable odor.

Prince, *Agaricus augustus*   EDIBLE, choice
Cap: 5–40 cm wide; convex with a flat center, aging to flat with an uplifted cap edge; covered with flat, yellowish brown to crust brown fibrils that converge to form scales; becoming yellow when bruised. Flesh thick, firm, white, turning pale yellow with age; odor sweet, like almonds or anise. **Gills:** Free of the stalk, closely spaced; white, turning pink and finally chocolate brown at maturity. **Stalk:** 8–20 cm long, 1.5–3.5 cm thick. Above the ring, it is white; below, it is covered with sheath-like fibrils and scales, white, becoming brownish with age. **Spore Print:** Chocolate brown. **Fruiting:** Solitary, scattered, or in small groups on the ground near trees, in cultivated areas; spring, summer, fall. **Range:** Western N. America; reported from Mich. **Family:** Agaricaceae. **Comments:** The large spores are distinctive. **Similar Species:** Wine-colored Agaricus (*A. subrutilescens*; edible, caution) has reddish brown cap fibrils and scales and occurs along the Pacific Coast; it causes gastrointestinal upset in some people. *A. subrufescens* (edible, choice), a primarily eastern species, has orange-brown cap fibrils and scales. Both are smaller and have cottony patches or zones of fibrils beneath the ring.

Agaricus fusco-fibrillosus   EDIBLE
Cap: 4–13 cm wide; convex, becoming flat with age; surface composed of flat, dark reddish brown radial fibrils that rarely converge to form indistinct, flat scales near the cap edge. Flesh thick, white, staining red where cut or bruised. **Gills:** Free of the stalk; pink, gradually becoming dark brown with age; with white edges. **Stalk:** 5–15 cm long, 8–25 mm thick, equal in thickness overall to club-shaped; smooth or nearly so; white, staining red where bruised; with a flaring, thin, membrane-like ring at or above the stalk center. **Spore Print:** Dark brown. **Fruiting:** Solitary, scattered, or in small groups under conifers or hardwoods, especially cypress and oak; fall, winter. **Range:** Central Calif. **Family:** Agaricaceae. **Comments:** One of several *Agaricus* species with red-staining flesh. **Similar Species:** Bleeding Agaricus (*A. haemorrhoidarius*; edible, caution) has a distinctly scaly cap and somewhat larger spores.

White Matsutake ▶
Tricholoma magnivelare

▼ Prince, *Agaricus augustus*

▼ *Agaricus fusco-fibrillosus*

MUSHROOMS WITH RING ONLY

RING MEMBRANOUS OR COTTONY

Eastern Flat-topped Agaric, *Agaricus placomyces* POISONOUS

Cap: 5–10 cm wide; convex to nearly flat with age; dry; white, becoming grayish brown at the center in maturity; covered with gray-brown to dark brown, hair-like scales. Flesh thick, firm, white to pinkish brown with age; bruising slowly yellow, then grayish red; odor unpleasant. **Gills:** Free of the stalk, crowded together; pale pink, aging to chocolate brown. **Stalk:** 4.5–15 cm long, 5–20 mm thick, becoming enlarged near the base; white, turning yellow when cut or bruised; with a white membranous ring. **Spore Print:** Dark brown. **Fruiting:** On the ground under conifers and hardwoods and on fertilized soil; late summer, fall. **Range:** Eastern N. America, west to the Great Plains. **Family:** Agaricaceae. **Comments:** Yellowish droplets may be present on the underside of the ring; these leave brown spots after drying. **Similar Species:** *A. pocillator* (edibility unknown) is nearly identical but has small, gray cap scales and a conspicuously double ring. Western Flat-topped Agaric (*A. meleagris*; poisonous) has large black scales on the cap and an unpleasant odor; it reaches 15 cm wide and is found on the West Coast. Yellow-foot Agaric (*A. xanthodermus*; poisonous) is white and quickly stains bright yellow when cut or bruised; it has an unpleasant odor.

Pink Bottom, *Agaricus campestris* EDIBLE, choice

Cap: 2.5–10 cm wide; convex to nearly flat with age; smooth, dry; white to grayish brown. Flesh thick, soft, white; taste mild. **Gills:** Free of the stalk, crowded together; pink when young, aging to dark brown. **Stalk:** 2.5–8 cm long, 5–20 mm thick; equal in thickness overall or narrowing near the base; white; with a white membranous ring. **Spore Print:** Dark brown. **Fruiting:** Solitary, scattered, or clustered on the ground on lawns, in pastures, on golf courses; summer, early fall. **Range:** Throughout N. America. **Family:** Agaricaceae. **Comments:** Be certain to check the spore print to rule out deadly *Amanita* species. **Similar Species:** Horse Mushroom (*Agaricus arvensis*; edible, choice) is larger, has an almond-like odor, and bruises yellow. Spring Agaricus (*Agaricus bitorquis*; edible, choice) has a double-edged ring on the stalk.

Smooth Lepiota, *Lepiota naucinoides* EDIBLE (caution)

Cap: 5–12 cm wide; egg-shaped when young, aging to convex to nearly flat; dry, smooth to slightly rough; white, sometimes with small, grayish white scales. Flesh thick, firm, white. **Gills:** Free of the stalk, closely spaced; white. **Stalk:** 5–12 cm long, 1–2 cm thick; nearly equal in thickness overall, becoming enlarged at the base; smooth to silky; white; with a white, membranous, thick-edged ring. **Spore Print:** White. **Fruiting:** Scattered or in groups in grassy areas; fall (also winter in Calif.). **Range:** Throughout N. America. **Family:** Lepiotaceae. **Comments:** Also known as *L. naucina*. Although this mushroom is a choice edible, some people have experienced gastric upset after eating it. Be careful not to confuse it with poisonous *Amanita* species. **Similar Species:** Destroying Angel (*Amanita virosa*; deadly) and several related species are white overall and have a sac-like cup at the base of the stalk and a white membranous ring with a thick edge.

▲ Eastern Flat-topped Agaric, *Agaricus placomyces*

▲ Pink Bottom, *Agaricus campestris*

▲ Smooth Lepiota, *Lepiota naucinoides*

MUSHROOMS WITH RING ONLY

RING MEMBRANOUS OR COTTONY

Spring Agrocybe, *Agrocybe praecox*   EDIBLE (caution)

Cap: 3–10 cm wide; convex to nearly flat with age, usually with a low knob; smooth to somewhat wrinkled; yellowish brown, darker near the center. Flesh moderately thick, firm, white. **Gills:** Attached to the stalk, closely spaced; dull white, aging to grayish brown. **Stalk:** 3–10 cm long, 5–15 mm thick; nearly equal in thickness overall; white to dull white or light brown; with a white membranous ring near the top. **Spore Print:** Brown. **Fruiting:** Scattered or in groups on the ground in hardwood and mixed forests, on lawns, and in gardens; spring, summer. **Range:** Widely distributed in N. America. **Family:** Bolbitiaceae. **Comments:** Although listed as edible, this mushroom can be difficult to recognize, and great care must be taken before eating it. **Similar Species:** Maple Agrocybe (*A. acericola*; edible) has a yellowish brown cap and a white stalk that ages to dark brown near the base; it fruits on hardwood debris during summer and fall. Hard Agrocybe (*A. dura*; edible) has a white to dull brown cap (often cracking with age), white gills that become brown with age, and a white stalk that typically lacks a ring; it grows on grass and among wood chips.

Hard's Stropharia, *Stropharia hardii*   EDIBILITY UNKNOWN

Cap: 2.5–10 cm wide; convex to nearly flat with age; dry; yellowish brown to golden brown, often with darker brown areas, especially toward the cap edge. Flesh thick, firm, dull white. **Gills:** Attached to the stalk, closely spaced; grayish brown, aging to purple-brown. **Stalk:** 5–7 cm long, 5–15 mm thick; nearly equal in thickness overall; white to pale yellowish brown; with a white membranous ring. **Spore Print:** Purple-brown. **Fruiting:** Solitary or in groups on the ground in hardwood forests; summer, fall. **Range:** Eastern N. America. **Family:** Strophariaceae. **Comments:** This mushroom usually has thick white threads at the point of attachment. **Similar Species:** Wine-cap Stropharia (*S. rugosoannulata*; edible) has a reddish brown to reddish purple cap, grayish gills, and a thick ring with grooves on the upper surface; it grows on wood chips. Lacerated Stropharia (*S. hornemannii*; edibility unknown) has a brownish cap with white scales and a white, cottony-scaly stalk below a skirt-like membranous ring; it grows on or near rotting conifer wood. Garland Stropharia (*S. coronilla*; poisonous) has a yellow cap and grows in fields and pastures.

Gypsy, *Rozites caperata*   EDIBLE, choice (caution)

Cap: 5–15 cm wide; egg-shaped to nearly flat with age; smooth, dry to somewhat moist; yellowish brown to orange-brown. Flesh moderately thick, firm, yellowish. **Gills:** Attached to the stalk, closely spaced; pale yellow, turning brown with maturity. **Stalk:** 5–12 cm long, 1–2 cm thick; becoming enlarged toward the base; pale yellowish brown; with a membranous ring near the apex. **Spore Print:** Rusty orange. **Fruiting:** Solitary to scattered, sometimes in groups, on the ground in conifer and hardwood forests; fall. **Range:** Northeastern and northwestern N. America and at higher elevations in the South. **Family:** Cortinariaceae. **Comments:** Use caution and be certain of your identification; many members of this family are poisonous. **Similar Species:** Bracelet Cort (*Cortinarius armillatus*; edible) has a reddish brown cap and a brownish stalk with reddish, bracelet-like bands and a bulbous base; young specimens have a cobwebby partial veil.

◀ Spring Agrocybe
Agrocybe praecox

▼ Hard's Stropharia
Stropharia hardii

▼ Gypsy
Rozites caperata

MUSHROOMS WITH RING ONLY

RING MEMBRANOUS OR COTTONY

Green-spored Lepiota, *Chlorophyllum molybdites* POISONOUS

Cap: 7–30 cm wide; convex to nearly flat with age; dry, dull; with pale brown center and scales on a white background. Flesh thick, firm, white, bruising orange and then reddish brown. **Gills:** Free of the stalk, closely spaced; white, becoming greenish with age. **Stalk:** 10–25 cm long, 1–2.5 cm thick, enlarging slightly near the base; white to creamy white, bruising reddish brown when handled; with a thick-edged, flaring, membranous, white ring. **Spore Print:** Pale green. **Fruiting:** Solitary to scattered on lawns and grasslands and along roadsides after heavy rains; late summer, fall. **Range:** Widely distributed but most common in southern areas. **Family:** Lepiotaceae. **Comments:** Can cause prolonged gastric distress, including severe diarrhea. **Similar Species:** Shaggy Parasol (*Lepiota rachodes*; edible, choice) and other species of *Lepiota* form white spore prints. *Amanita* species form white spore prints and have a cup at the base of the stalk. *Agaricus* and *Stropharia* species form brown or purple-brown spore prints.

Shaggy Parasol, *Lepiota rachodes* EDIBLE, choice (caution)

Cap: 5–20 cm wide; convex to nearly flat with age; dry; with dull brown center and coarse scales on a white background. Flesh thick, firm, white, bruising orange and then reddish brown. **Gills:** Free of the stalk, closely spaced; white. **Stalk:** 5–15 cm long, 1–2 cm thick, enlarging near the base; white, shading to pale brown on the lower portion; with a flaring, thick-edged, white ring toward the apex. **Spore Print:** White. **Fruiting:** Solitary or in groups on the ground among leaves, needles, and wood chips and in gardens; summer, fall (also winter in Calif.). **Range:** Throughout N. America. **Family:** Lepiotaceae. **Comments:** Do not confuse it with the poisonous Green-spored Lepiota. **Similar Species:** Parasol (*L. procera*; edible, choice) has a long, slender, scaly stalk; its flesh does not turn orange when cut. Green-spored Lepiota (*Chlorophyllum molybdites*; poisonous) has a similarly colored cap with smaller, looser, more fragile scales; it forms a pale green spore print. *Lepiota americana* (edible) is reddish brown, has a spindle-shaped stalk, and grows in clusters.

Reddening Lepiota, *Lepiota americana* EDIBLE (caution)

Cap: 3–15 cm wide; narrowly convex at first, becoming convex and finally flat with age, with a central knob; minutely grooved at the cap edge; with a dull reddish brown center and concentric scales on a white background; white areas bruising yellow and then slowly reddish brown. Flesh thin, soft, fragile; white, bruising yellow, then becoming orange and finally reddish brown. **Gills:** Free of the stalk, closely spaced; fragile; white, with a bruising pattern like the cap's, but the reddish brown color slowly disappears. **Stalk:** 7–14 cm long, 8–22 mm thick; tapered both above and at the base or club-shaped; smooth; white, with a bruising pattern like the cap's; with a membranous, white ring, thickened at the edge. **Spore Print:** White. **Fruiting:** Scattered or in clusters (rarely solitary) near stumps, among wood chips, or in sawdust and in gardens and on lawns; summer, fall. **Range:** Throughout N. America, but rare in the West. **Family:** Lepiotaceae. **Comments:** This species turns wine red when cooked or dried. **Similar Species:** Green-spored Lepiota (*Chlorophyllum molybdites*; poisonous) and the white-spored Shaggy Parasol (*Lepiota rachodes*; edible, choice) are both thicker-fleshed and more robust.

Green-spored
Lepiota ▶
*Chlorophyllum
molybdites*

▼ Shaggy Parasol, *Lepiota rachodes*

Reddening
Lepiota ▶
Lepiota americana

MUSHROOMS WITH RING ONLY

RING MEMBRANOUS OR COTTONY

Honey Mushroom, *Armillariella mellea*   EDIBLE, choice

Cap: 2.5–12 cm wide; convex to nearly flat with age; sticky to slippery when wet; yellowish brown to pinkish brown; with few to several short, erect, brown hairs covering the cap center. Flesh thick, firm, white. **Gills:** Attached to the stalk, somewhat separated, partially descending the stalk. **Stalk:** 5–15 cm long, 1–2 cm thick, equal in thickness overall; yellowish brown to pinkish brown; with a membranous white ring near the apex. **Spore Print:** White. **Fruiting:** Solitary or in fused clusters on trees, stumps, and buried wood; fall. **Range:** Throughout N. America. **Family:** Tricholomataceae. **Comments:** Also known as *Armillaria mellea*. This mushroom is a complex of several closely related species that are distinguished by microscopic and other technical features. **Similar Species:** Ringless Honey Mushroom (*A. tabescens;* edible) is also found on wood (often buried wood), but it lacks a ring and has a dry cap. Deadly Galerina (*Galerina autumnalis;* deadly) is smaller, has a thin ring that often falls off, and forms a rusty brown spore print.

Magic Mushroom, *Psilocybe cubensis*   POISONOUS (hallucinogenic)

Cap: 1.5–8 cm wide; conical, aging to bell-shaped, then convex, and finally flat, with a central knob; smooth, sticky; white, aging to pale yellow and finally pale brown, bruising or aging blue. Flesh solid, white, bruising blue. **Gills:** Attached to the stalk, closely spaced; grayish to violet-gray, mottled; blackening with age; with white edges. **Stalk:** 4–15 cm long, 4–14 mm thick, equal in thickness overall, enlarged toward the base; with vertical lines at the apex, smooth below; off-white, bruising blue where handled; interior hollow; upper part of stalk with a white, flaring ring that becomes dark on its upper surface from accumulation of spores. **Spore Print:** Purple-brown. **Fruiting:** Solitary or more often in groups on horse or cow dung; year-round. **Range:** Fla. and the Gulf Coast. **Family:** Strophariaceae. **Comments:** Contains the hallucinogenic compounds psilocybin and psilocin, which affect the central nervous system. **Similar Species:** The smaller (1–2 cm wide) Dung-loving Psilocybe (*P. coprophila;* poisonous, hallucinogenic) also occurs on dung but does not form a well-developed ring.

Stropharia squamosa* var. *thrausta   POISONOUS

Cap: 3–8 cm wide; convex, aging to broadly convex; with a shallow central knob; sticky when wet; with scattered, superficial scales (especially near the cap edge); orange to brick red. Flesh solid, firm, white. **Gills:** Attached to the stalk, closely spaced; pale, becoming grayish to violet-brown with age; edges white. **Stalk:** 6–12 cm long, 3–6 mm thick, equal in thickness overall; coarsely scaly below; off-white; with a well-developed, flaring, white ring toward the apex. **Spore Print:** Purple-brown. **Fruiting:** Scattered or in groups on buried wood and woody debris of conifers and hardwoods. **Range:** Eastern N. America. **Family:** Strophariaceae. **Comments:** Caps of the typical and widespread variety, *S. squamosa* var. *squamosa* (poisonous), are chestnut brown to dull yellow but are otherwise similar. **Similar Species:** Questionable Stropharia (*S. ambigua;* edible) of the Pacific Northwest is larger, yellow, and sticky when wet; it has a poorly developed ring.

▲ Honey Mushroom, *Armillariella mellea*

▲ Magic Mushroom
Psilocybe cubensis

Stropharia squamosa var. *thrausta* ▶

MUSHROOMS WITH RING ONLY

RING MEMBRANOUS OR COTTONY

Red-tinged Lepiota, *Lepiota rubrotincta*   EDIBILITY UNKNOWN

Cap: 2–8 cm wide; narrowly convex, aging to convex, then flat, and finally uplifted at the margin; sometimes with a low central knob; dull red to pinkish red, darker in the center; smooth overall at first, often splitting radially toward the margin and exposing the white flesh. Flesh relatively thin, fragile, white. **Gills:** Free of the stalk, closely spaced; white. **Stalk:** 4–20 cm long, 4–10 mm thick, equal in thickness overall or enlarged and club-shaped toward the base; smooth, white; interior stuffed, aging to hollow; with a fragile, white membranous ring. **Spore Print:** White. **Fruiting:** Solitary or scattered in soil and humus under hardwoods and conifers; summer, fall. **Range:** Throughout N. America. **Family:** Lepiotaceae. **Similar Species:** *L. glabridisca* (edibility unknown) is of similar stature but has a distinct purplish brown (not red) cast to the cap; it is restricted to the Pacific Northwest.

Unspotted Cystoderma, *Cystoderma amianthinum*   EDIBLE

Cap: 1.5–4.5 cm wide; convex to nearly flat with age; dry, finely wrinkled, granular; often with cottony, white tissue hanging from the cap edge; yellow-brown. Flesh thin, soft, white. **Gills:** Attached to or somewhat notched at the stalk, closely spaced; yellowish orange to yellowish brown. **Stalk:** 2.5–6.5 cm long, 2–8 mm thick, nearly equal in thickness overall; coloration like the cap's; with a white fibrous ring that often disappears with age and white fibers scattered over the lower portion below the ring. **Spore Print:** White. **Fruiting:** Solitary or in groups on the ground (often among mosses) under conifers; late summer, fall. **Range:** Widely distributed in N. America. **Family:** Tricholomataceae. **Similar Species:** Pungent Cystoderma (*C. amianthinum* var. *rugusoreticulatum*; edibility unknown) has a wrinkled and granular, yellow-brown cap and a sheath-like, yellow-brown ring; it exhibits a strong odor. Common Conifer Cystoderma (*C. fallax*; edibility unknown) has a granular, rust brown cap and a rust brown, sock-like ring; it lacks a strong odor.

Deadly Lepiota, *Lepiota helveola*   DEADLY

Cap: 1.3–5 cm wide; convex, aging to nearly flat, often with a broad, central knob; minutely hairy; with chestnut brown to cinnamon to pinkish cinnamon center and concentric scales on a white to pinkish background. Flesh thick at the center (thin elsewhere), fragile, white; odor sweet, pleasant. **Gills:** Free of the stalk, closely spaced; white, aging to pale cream. **Stalk:** 3.5–9 cm long, 3–8 mm thick, ranging from equal in thickness overall to nearly club-shaped; silky smooth above; off-white to pinkish white; covered toward the base with small, elongated, pad-like scales with surface coloration like the cap's; ring present only as the upper zone of pad-like scales. **Spore Print:** White. **Fruiting:** Solitary to scattered in soil and humus under hardwoods and conifers; fall. **Range:** Apparently widely distributed: Pacific Coast and reported from N.Y., Ill., and Ky. **Family:** Lepiotaceae. **Comments:** This and several other *Lepiota* species with pad-like stalk scales (such as *L. josserandii*) contain amatoxins and are deadly. **Similar Species:** *L. felina* (edibility unknown) has dark brown cap and stalk scales. Malodorous Lepiota (*L. cristata*; poisonous) has a scaly, reddish brown cap and lacks hairs; it has a farinaceous (metallic-mealy) taste and often a disagreeable odor.

▲ Red-tinged Lepiota, *Lepiota rubrotincta*

▲ Unspotted Cystoderma, *Cystoderma amianthinum*

▼ Deadly Lepiota, *Lepiota helveola*

MUSHROOMS WITH RING ONLY

RING FIBROUS

Shaggy Mane, Coprinus comatus   EDIBLE, choice

Cap: 2.5–5 cm wide; oval to cylindrical, aging to convex or bell-shaped; dry; with shallow grooves near the edge; white, with reddish brown scales. Flesh soft, white. **Gills:** Free of the stalk, very crowded together; white when very young, becoming gray, then black, and dissolving away with age. **Stalk:** 5–20 cm long, 1–2.5 cm thick, becoming enlarged downward; white; interior hollow; with a white, ring-like zone of fibers near the base. **Spore Print:** Black. **Fruiting:** Solitary, scattered, or clustered on lawns, in pastures, and along roadsides; spring, fall, early winter. **Range:** Throughout N. America. **Family:** Coprinaceae. **Comments:** Unless cooked, this mushroom, like other inky caps, will dissolve into a black fluid, even if refrigerated. **Similar Species:** C. sterquilinus (edibility unknown) is smaller and pure white; it grows on dung. C. brassicae (edibility unknown) is less than 1 cm tall and white; it grows attached to grass and plant debris. Scaly Inky Cap (C. variegatus = C. quadrifidus; edibility not clearly established) is grayish brown with rusty brown patches; it grows in dense clusters on lawns and rotting wood.

Coprinus laniger   EDIBILITY UNKNOWN

Cap: 1–2.5 cm wide; thin, conical to bell-shaped, yellowish brown to grayish brown; with grooves near the cap edge; covered with yellowish brown scales that easily wash off. Flesh thin, fragile, yellowish. **Gills:** Attached to the stalk, crowded together; white when young, aging to gray and finally black; dissolving with age. **Stalk:** 1–2.5 cm long, 2–4 mm thick, slightly enlarged near the base; white to dull yellow; interior hollow; with a white fibrous ring. **Spore Print:** Black. **Fruiting:** Scattered or in groups on decaying wood; summer, fall. **Range:** Widely distributed in eastern N. America. **Family:** Coprinaceae. **Comments:** The base of the stalk is embedded in a thick mat of orange threads. **Similar Species:** Orange-mat Coprinus (C. radians; edibility unknown) has a larger, egg-shaped to bell-shaped, brownish cap with scurfy scales; it also exhibits a mat of orange threads at the stalk base and grows on decaying wood.

Alcohol Inky, Coprinus atramentarius   EDIBLE (caution)

Cap: 5–8 cm wide; oval to convex with age; smooth, dry; gray to gray-brown; with shallow grooves near the edge. Flesh thin, firm, grayish white. **Gills:** Free of the stalk, very crowded together; white when very young, then turning gray, becoming black and dissolving with age. **Stalk:** 3–15 cm long, 1–2.5 cm thick; white; interior hollow; with a ring-like zone of white fibers near the base. **Spore Print:** Black. **Fruiting:** In clusters on grass, wood chips, and tree bases; late spring, summer, fall (also winter in Calif.). **Range:** Throughout N. America. **Family:** Coprinaceae. **Comments:** This is an excellent edible, but some persons have experienced nausea, vomiting, and a flushed feeling following consumption with alcohol (the alcohol does not have to be consumed at the same time as the mushroom). **Similar Species:** Shaggy Mane (C. comatus; edible, choice) is white with reddish brown scales. Mica Cap (C. micaceus; edible) has a much shorter stalk and a yellow-brown to reddish brown cap; it grows in dense clusters.

◀ Shaggy Mane
Coprinus comatus

Coprinus laniger ▶

Alcohol Inky ▶
*Coprinus
atramentarius*

MUSHROOMS WITH RING ONLY

RING FIBROUS

Sharp-Scaly Pholiota, *Pholiota squarrosoides*   EDIBLE (caution)

Cap: 2–10 cm wide; convex to nearly flat with age; sometimes with a low knob; sticky when wet; pale yellow to yellow-brown; covered with flattened or erect, sharply pointed, yellow-brown scales. Flesh thick, firm, white. **Gills:** Attached to the stalk, somewhat separated; creamy white, aging to rusty brown; covered with a scaly, yellowish brown veil in young specimens. **Stalk:** 5–12 cm long, 5–15 mm thick; yellowish brown; with a membranous or hairy ring; smooth above the ring and covered with coarse, yellow-brown to reddish brown scales below. **Spore Print:** Brown. **Fruiting:** In clusters on decaying conifer and hardwood trees, stumps, and logs; summer, fall. **Range:** Widely distributed in N. America. **Family:** Strophariaceae. **Comments:** Easily confused with other *Pholiota* species, some of which are reported to cause gastric distress. **Similar Species:** Scaly Pholiota (*P. squarrosa*; poisonous) has a dry cap with coarse, flattened scales. *P. aurivella* (edible) has a yellowish orange cap with large, flattened, reddish scales.

Scalloped Pholiota, *Pholiota albocrenulata*   EDIBILITY UNKNOWN

Cap: 2.5–8 cm wide; convex to nearly flat with age; slimy; orange-brown to reddish brown, often with flattened, brown scales; with white patches of tissue hanging from the cap edge. Flesh thick, firm, dull white. **Gills:** Attached to or notched at the stalk, closely spaced; white, becoming gray with age; edges white and finely notched. **Stalk:** 3–8 cm long, 5–15 mm thick, enlarging slightly near the base; yellowish brown, covered with reddish brown fibers and scales; with a delicate fibrous ring. **Spore Print:** Brown. **Fruiting:** Solitary or in groups on decaying wood; fall. **Range:** Widely distributed in N. America. **Family:** Strophariaceae. **Similar Species:** Destructive Pholiota (*P. destruens*; edible) has a very large, sticky, creamy white to pale brown cap with dull brownish scales; it exhibits a white to pale brown stalk and a fibrous ring and grows on the ends of dead hardwood limbs and logs. Yellow Pholiota (*P. flammans*; edibility unknown) has a slimy, scaly, yellow cap and bright yellow gills and stalk; it grows on decaying wood.

Big Laughing Gym, *Gymnopilus spectabilis*
POISONOUS (hallucinogenic)

Cap: 8–16 cm wide; convex to nearly flat with age; smooth, slippery when wet; yellow-orange to orange-brown. Flesh thick, firm, yellow; odor of anise; taste very bitter. **Gills:** Attached to the stalk, closely spaced; yellowish orange to rusty brown. **Stalk:** 5–20 cm long, 1–3 cm thick, equal in thickness overall or slightly enlarged at the base; yellowish brown with dark brown streaks; with a thin, fibrous, yellowish ring. **Spore Print:** Rusty orange. **Fruiting:** In clusters on trees or buried wood; fall. **Range:** Widely distributed in N. America. **Family:** Cortinariaceae. **Comments:** Ingestion of this mushroom has been reported to cause irrational laughter. **Similar Species:** Little Gym (*G. penetrans*; edibility unknown) has a smaller, yellow cap and a yellowish stalk; it grows on wood. *Pholiota malicola* var. *malicola* (edibility unknown) has a yellowish orange cap with brown fibers, and its stalk has a yellowish, fibrous ring; it lacks an anise odor and exhibits a mild taste; it grows in clusters on decaying wood. *P. malicola* var. *macropoda* (edibility unknown) is nearly identical to var. *malicola* but exhibits an odor of fresh corn.

▲ Sharp-Scaly Pholiota, *Pholiota squarrosoides*

▲ Scalloped Pholiota, *Pholiota albocrenulata*

▲ Big Laughing Gym, *Gymnopilus spectabilis*

MUSHROOMS WITH RING ONLY

RING FIBROUS

Violet Cort, *Cortinarius violaceus*   EDIBLE

Cap: 5–15 cm wide; round at first, aging to convex or nearly flat; with a broad, low knob and minute, pointed scales in the center and a radial arrangement of fibrils and scales elsewhere; dark violet. Flesh thick, dark violet. **Gills:** Attached to the stalk, somewhat separated; dark violet, aging to dull violet-brown. **Stalk:** 7–16 cm long, 1–2.5 cm thick, equal in thickness overall or tapered toward the apex; surface with scattered fibrils; dark violet; with a cobwebby partial veil that leaves a hairy ring of fibrils near the apex. **Spore Print:** Dark and dull rusty brown. **Fruiting:** Solitary to scattered under conifers; fall. **Range:** Northern N. America and at higher elevations in the South. **Family:** Cortinariaceae. **Comments:** The color and stature make this mushroom distinctive. **Similar Species:** Silvery Violet Cort (*C. alboviolaceus;* edible) is paler—uniformly silvery lilac—and silky-smooth. Viscid Violet Cort (*C. iodes;* edible) is slimy, with paler lilac to purple coloration. Violet Entoloma (*Entoloma violaceum;* edibility unknown) has a dry, scaly, violet cap and white gills that become pinkish with age; it forms a pinkish spore print.

Cortinarius corrugatus   EDIBILITY UNKNOWN

Cap: 3–10 cm wide; bell-shaped to convex, becoming nearly flat with age; sticky, shiny, smooth to slippery; with coarse wrinkles, yellow-brown to red-brown. Flesh thin, firm, white. **Gills:** Attached to the stalk, closely spaced; initially purple, aging to purple-cinnamon. **Stalk:** 6–8 cm long, 5–15 mm thick, enlarging near the base; yellowish, covered with brownish fibers; supporting a delicate fibrous ring that often disappears. **Spore Print:** Dull rusty brown. **Fruiting:** Solitary or scattered on the ground under hardwoods; summer, fall. **Range:** Widely distributed in eastern N. America. **Family:** Cortinariaceae. **Comments:** The combination of coarsely wrinkled, yellow-brown to red-brown cap and purple to purple-cinnamon gills makes this *Cortinarius* species easy to identify. **Similar Species:** Corrugated-cap Milky (*Lactarius corrugis;* edible) has a wrinkled, reddish brown cap and exudes a white latex when cut; it forms a white spore print. Corrugated-cap Psathyrella (*Psathyrella rugocephala;* edible) has a brown cap that is deeply wrinkled, nearly black gills, a white to brownish stalk, and a fibrous ring; it forms a purple-brown spore print.

Viscid Violet Cort, *Cortinarius iodes*   EDIBLE

Cap: 2.5–8 cm wide; convex to nearly flat with age; smooth, sticky; purple, with yellow spots near the center; surface mild-tasting. Flesh thin, firm, whitish. **Gills:** Attached to the stalk, closely spaced; purple in young specimens, aging to rusty brown. **Stalk:** 5–10 cm long, 5–10 mm thick, enlarging toward the base; white, covered with scant purple fibers; with a pale violet to rusty brown fibrous ring. **Spore Print:** Dull rusty brown. **Fruiting:** Solitary or in groups on the ground in hardwood forests; late summer, fall. **Range:** Widely distributed in N. America. **Family:** Cortinariaceae. **Comments:** Although listed as edible, this mushroom has a less than exciting flavor. **Similar Species:** *C. iodeoides* (inedible) has a bitter-tasting cap surface. Violet Cort (*C. violaceus;* edible) has a dry, scaly, dark purple cap and stalk. Pungent Cort (*C. traganus;* edibility unknown) has a dry, light purple cap and stalk and a disagreeable odor.

Violet Cort ▶
Cortinarius violaceus

▲ *Cortinarius corrugatus*

Viscid
  Violet Cort ▶
Cortinarius iodes

MUSHROOMS WITH RING ONLY

RING FIBROUS

Lilac Fiber Head, *Inocybe lilacina* POISONOUS

Cap: 2–4 cm wide; conical, aging to bell-shaped and finally convex to nearly flat, with a broad central knob; dry and silky-smooth; violet to lilac, fading to dull cream, but retaining some lilac tints; color does not change when tissues are bruised. Flesh solid, pallid; odor and taste unpleasant. **Gills:** Attached to the stalk, closely spaced; pallid to pale lilac, becoming brownish-tinged with age. **Stalk:** 4–6 cm long, 4–7 mm thick, equal in thickness overall; with a small basal bulb; apex lilac-tinged, paler and more pallid below; with a cobwebby veil that leaves a poorly developed fibrous ring. **Spore Print:** Brown. **Fruiting:** Solitary to scattered under hardwoods and conifers; late summer, fall. **Range:** Throughout N. America. **Family:** Cortinariaceae. **Comments:** Also known as *I. geophylla* var. *lilacina.* **Similar Species:** White Fiber Head (*I. geophylla;* poisonous) does not exhibit a coloration change when bruised. Blushing Fiber Head (*I. pudica;* poisonous) bruises red. Both are white and lack the violet to lilac coloration.

Brick Cap, *Naematoloma sublateritium* EDIBLE

Cap: 2.5–10 cm wide; convex to nearly flat with age; smooth; brick red with yellow-orange near the edge. Flesh thick, pale yellowish brown; taste mild. **Gills:** Attached to the stalk, closely spaced; pale yellow in young specimens, grayish purple in older ones. **Stalk:** 5–10 cm long, 5–15 mm thick; pale yellow, covered with reddish brown fibers; with a yellowish brown ring of fibers near the apex. **Spore Print:** Purple-brown. **Fruiting:** In clusters on hardwood stumps and logs; fall. **Range:** Eastern N. America, south into Mexico. **Family:** Strophariaceae. **Comments:** Also known as *Hypholoma sublateritium.* Although this species is an excellent edible, older specimens have tough stalks and less flavor. **Similar Species:** Smoky-gilled Naematoloma (*N. capnoides;* edible) has a yellowish orange cap, grayish to purple-brown gills, and a mild taste; it grows on decaying conifer wood. Sulphur Tuft (*N. fasciculare;* poisonous) has a yellow to yellow-brown cap and a bitter taste; young specimens have greenish yellow gills, which age to purple-brown.

Sulphur Tuft, *Naematoloma fasciculare* POISONOUS

Cap: 2–8 cm wide; convex to nearly flat with age; sometimes with a broad, low knob; smooth; greenish yellow to yellowish orange. Flesh moderately thick, pale yellow, bruising brown; taste very bitter. **Gills:** Attached to the stalk, closely spaced; yellow to greenish yellow, aging to purple-brown. **Stalk:** 5–12 cm long, 3–10 mm thick, narrowing slightly toward the base; pale yellow, aging to yellowish brown. **Spore Print:** Purple-brown. **Fruiting:** In clusters on hardwood logs and stumps; summer, fall. **Range:** Widely distributed in N. America. **Family:** Strophariaceae. **Comments:** Also known as *Hypholoma fasciculare.* The bitter taste remains after cooking. This species is known to cause gastric distress. **Similar Species:** Brick Cap (*N. sublateritium;* edible) has brick red caps and grayish purple gills. Smoky-gilled Naematoloma (*N. capnoides;* edible) has a yellowish orange cap and grayish to purple-brown gills; it grows on decaying conifer wood. Both have a mild taste.

▲ Lilac Fiber Head, *Inocybe lilacina*

▲ Brick Cap, *Naematoloma sublateritium*

▼ Sulphur Tuft, *Naematoloma fasciculare*

MUSHROOMS WITH RING ONLY
RING FIBROUS

Psathyrella septentrionalis   EDIBILITY UNKNOWN

Cap: 1.5–5 cm wide; convex to nearly flat with age; smooth to faintly grooved near the edge; moist; reddish brown when young, aging to cinnamon brown; with tooth-shaped patches of white veil attached to the edge. Flesh thin, fragile, water-soaked, brown to tan. **Gills:** Attached to the stalk, closely spaced; pale brown, aging to dark brown. **Stalk:** 1.5–6 cm long, 1.5–4 mm thick, nearly equal in thickness overall; nearly smooth; white, aging to honey brown. **Spore Print:** Brownish black. **Fruiting:** In clusters and groups on hardwood logs; summer, fall. **Range:** Widespread in N. America. **Family:** Coprinaceae. **Comments:** The moist, reddish brown caps in clusters with white, tooth-shaped veil patches on the edge are characteristic. **Similar Species:** Clustered Psathyrella (*P. hydrophila;* edibility unknown) is nearly identical but lacks the white, tooth-like veil patches and has smaller spores. Corrugated-cap Psathyrella (*P. rugocephala;* edible) is larger, has a deeply wrinkled cap, and grows on wood. *P. delineata* (edibility unknown) is similar to *P. rugocephala* but is smaller and has smaller spores.

Weeping Widow, *Psathyrella velutina*   EDIBLE

Cap: 2–12 cm wide; nearly spherical at first, aging to convex and finally nearly flat, usually with a central knob; covered with dense, flattened fibrils, many of which aggregate into scales; dark yellowish brown to orange-brown, paler toward the cap edge, which in young specimens is irregularly fringed with pallid remnants of a partial veil. Flesh thick, water-soaked, yellowish brown. **Gills:** Attached to the stalk, closely spaced; light to dark brown, mottled; edges white, with bead-like drops in young specimens. **Stalk:** 3–13 cm long, 3–15 mm thick, equal in thickness overall; yellowish brown with dull orange-brown fibrils and flattened scales below the ring, smooth and pallid above; ring present as a thin zone of hairy fibrils on the upper part of the stalk. **Spore Print:** Blackish brown. **Fruiting:** Solitary, scattered, or in small clusters in grassy areas and on organic debris, often at the edges of woods or in shrubby cultivated areas; summer, fall (also spring in Calif.). **Range:** Throughout N. America. **Family:** Coprinaceae. **Comments:** Also known as *Lacrymaria velutina.* **Similar Species:** The fibrils and flattened scales are reminiscent of some *Inocybe* species, all of which form brown spore prints.

Deadly Galerina, *Galerina autumnalis*   DEADLY

Cap: 2.5–6 cm wide, convex to nearly flat with age; smooth, moist, sticky; yellow-brown to chestnut brown. Flesh thick, firm, water-soaked, pale brown. **Gills:** Attached to the stalk, closely spaced; yellowish brown to rusty brown. **Stalk:** 2.5–10 cm long, 3–10 mm thick; white on the upper portion, brown on the lower portion; with a narrow, white, fibrous ring that often disappears. **Spore Print:** Rusty brown. **Fruiting:** Solitary or in groups on rotting logs and stumps of conifers and hardwoods; spring, summer, fall. **Range:** Throughout N. America. **Family:** Cortinariaceae. **Comments:** This mushroom can cause liver and kidney damage, coma, and death. Beware of "Little Brown Mushrooms"! **Similar Species:** Deadly Lawn Galerina (*G. venenata;* deadly) has a reddish brown cap, is smaller, grows on lawns, and is restricted to Wash. and Ore. Little Gym (*Gymnopilus penetrans;* edibility unknown) has a yellowish orange to yellowish brown cap, a yellowish stalk, and a delicate, whitish veil covering the gills of young specimens.

▲ *Psathyrella septentrionalis*

▲ Weeping Widow, *Psathyrella velutina*

▲ Deadly Galerina, *Galerina autumnalis*

MUSHROOMS WITH RING ONLY

RING FIBROUS

Armillaria olida   EDIBILITY UNKNOWN

Cap: 7–15 cm wide; convex, aging to flat; cap edge aging to wavy, irregular in outline, and sometimes elevated; smooth, dull; whitish when young, aging to grayish olive to grayish brown. Flesh thick, white; strong odor of rotting potatoes; taste farinaceous (metallic-mealy) and disagreeable. **Gills:** Attached to the stalk, tearing free with age; closely spaced; white, with a slight pinkish cast in older specimens. **Stalk:** 8–14 cm long, 2–3.5 cm wide; ranging from equal in thickness overall to nearly club-shaped at the base; smooth or with scattered, appressed fibrils; white, sometimes with a slight olive cast; ring thin, white, fibrous, at or above the mid-stalk. **Spore Print:** White. **Fruiting:** Solitary to scattered in humus under conifers at higher elevations; late spring, early summer. **Range:** Sierra Nevada of Calif.; rare in the northern California Coast Ranges. **Family:** Tricholomataceae. **Comments:** This species is often associated with melting snowpacks. **Similar Species:** Stature and color are suggestive of some species of *Lyophyllum*, but there are differences in anatomy.

Woolly Chroogomphus, *Chroogomphus tomentosus*   EDIBLE

Cap: 2–6 cm wide; broadly convex, aging to flat; dry, covered with radially arranged, woolly fibrils that aggregate to form scales; pale orange to yellowish orange. Flesh thick at the center, firm, orange-yellow to pale salmon. **Gills:** Attached to and descending the stalk, somewhat separated; pale orange to yellowish orange, becoming grayish orange to smoky brown (blackish) as the spores mature. **Stalk:** 4–17 cm long, 9–14 mm thick, tapering at the base; surface covered with thin fibrils, with coloration like the cap's; interior solid; flesh yellowish orange to pale salmon; with a thin, indistinct, fibrous ring near the stalk apex. **Spore Print:** Grayish black. **Fruiting:** Solitary, scattered, or in small groups in humus under conifers; fall. **Range:** Pacific Northwest. **Family:** Gomphidiaceae. **Comments:** Also known as *Gomphidius tomentosus*. Very common in mountain conifer forests of the West. **Similar Species:** *Chroogomphus leptocystis* (edible) has a more reddish brown cap color and smaller spores; other species in the genus are smooth and sticky.

Wine-cap Chroogomphus, *Chroogomphus vinicolor*   EDIBLE

Cap: 1–12 cm wide; nearly spherical before opening, aging to convex and finally nearly flat, with a central knob; sticky, smooth, often shiny; orange-red to dull wine red. Flesh thick, solid, orange-yellow to pale salmon. **Gills:** Attached to and descending the stalk; somewhat separated; pale orange to yellowish orange, becoming grayish orange to smoky brown (blackish) as the spores mature. **Stalk:** 5–10 cm long, 6–20 mm thick, tapering toward the base; smooth; orange-red to dull wine red; interior solid, flesh tinged orange-yellow to pale salmon; with a thin, indistinct fibrous ring near the stalk apex. **Spore Print:** Grayish black. **Fruiting:** Occasionally solitary, more frequently scattered or in small clusters under conifers; late summer, fall (summer to early spring in coastal Calif.). **Range:** Widespread in N. America. **Family:** Gomphidiaceae. **Comments:** Also known as *Gomphidius vinicolor*. **Similar Species:** Brownish Chroogomphus (*Chroogomphus rutilus*; edible) is also sticky but has a more reddish brown color, occasionally with grayish overtones; it is sometimes difficult to distinguish without a microscope.

Armillaria olida ▶

▼ Woolly Chroogomphus
Chroogomphus tomentosus

▼ Wine-cap Chroogomphus, *Chroogomphus vinicolor*

MUSHROOMS WITH RING ONLY

RING STICKY

Rosy Gomphidius, *Gomphidius subroseus*   EDIBLE

Cap: 4–6 cm wide; convex to nearly flat with age; smooth, slimy when wet; pinkish red to red. Flesh thick, firm, white. **Gills:** Partially descending the stalk, somewhat separated; white, becoming smoky gray in older specimens; covered by a thin, colorless, sticky veil in young specimens. **Stalk:** 3–7 cm long, 5–17 mm thick, nearly equal in thickness overall or tapering toward the base; white and silky above a sticky ring, creamy white below, yellow near the base. **Spore Print:** Black. **Fruiting:** Solitary to scattered under conifers; summer, fall. **Range:** Widely distributed in N. America. **Family:** Gomphidiaceae. **Comments:** Although found in the East, this is primarily a western species. **Similar Species:** Spotted Gomphidius (*G. maculatus;* edible) has a pinkish brown cap, lacks a veil, and becomes black with age or injury. Slimy Gomphidius (*G. glutinosus;* edible) has a slimy, gray-brown or purplish cap; its fruiting pattern is solitary to scattered. *G. oregonensis* (edible) has a slimy, pinkish to reddish brown cap; it occurs in tight clusters. Both *G. glutinosus* and *G. oregonensis* have grayish gills and a slimy ring; they are best identified by spore size.

Cortinarius salor   EDIBILITY UNKNOWN

Cap: 4–7 cm wide; convex, aging to nearly flat with a slight depression at the center; slimy, smooth; bright violet to bluish violet, fading to rusty red and then apricot; paler near the cap edge. Flesh thick, firm, bluish purple or paler. **Gills:** Attached to or partially descending the stalk, somewhat separated; lilac to violet, aging to coffee brown. **Stalk:** 4–12 cm long, 5–20 mm thick, nearly equal in thickness overall or enlarging somewhat near the base; pale violet or grayish white with tawny streaks; with a sticky ring. **Spore Print:** Dull rusty brown. **Fruiting:** Solitary or scattered on the ground in conifer and hardwood forests; summer, fall. **Range:** Eastern N. America. **Family:** Cortinariaceae. **Comments:** Little is known about the distribution of this mushroom; its range may be wider than stated. **Similar Species:** *C. cylindripes* (edibility unknown) has a slimy, lavender cap that ages to reddish brown and has short radial lines near the cap edge; its spores are much larger.

Slimy-veil Limacella, *Limacella glioderma*   EDIBILITY UNKNOWN

Cap: 2–7 cm wide; convex to nearly flat with age, with a broad, low knob; slimy; reddish brown near the center, orange-brown toward the cap edge. Flesh thick, firm, white; odor and taste farinaceous (metallic-mealy) and unpleasant. **Gills:** Free of the stalk or nearly so; closely spaced; white. **Stalk:** 5–10 cm long, 5–10 mm thick; smooth or somewhat cottony; reddish brown or paler; with a slightly sticky, hairy ring; with sticky patches below the ring when wet. **Spore Print:** White. **Fruiting:** Solitary or in groups on the ground in mixed woods; fall. **Range:** Widely distributed in N. America. **Family:** Amanitaceae. **Comments:** Formerly known as *Lepiota glioderma.* The color in older specimens fades to pinkish brown. **Similar Species:** Ringed Limacella (*Limacella solidipes;* edibility unknown) has a sticky, cream white cap and a large, white, membranous ring. *Limacella glischra* (edibility unknown) has a yellow-brown cap, a white to pale yellow-brown stalk, and a slimy, hairy ring.

▲ Rosy Gomphidius, *Gomphidius subroseus*

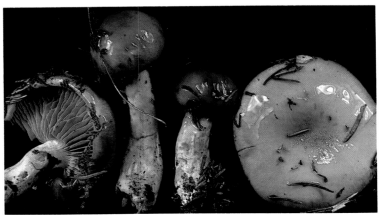

▲ *Cortinarius salor*

▲ Slimy-veil Limacella, *Limacella glioderma*

SMALL FRAGILE MUSHROOMS

Zoned-cap Collybia, *Crinipellis zonata*   EDIBILITY UNKNOWN

Cap: 1–2.5 cm wide; convex to nearly flat with age, sometimes depressed at the center; covered with dark brown to yellow-brown hairs and typically with rings of darker and lighter color; cap edge inrolled in young specimens. Flesh thin, firm, white. **Gills:** Free of the stalk, closely spaced; white. **Stalk:** 2.5–5 cm long, 1–2 mm thick, nearly equal in thickness overall; covered with dark brown to yellow-brown hairs. **Spore Print:** White. **Fruiting:** Solitary or in clusters on decaying hardwood twigs; fall. **Range:** Eastern N. America. **Family:** Tricholomataceae. **Comments:** Formerly known as *Collybia zonata.* The yellow-brown hairs turn reddish in Melzer's solution. **Similar Species:** *Crinipellis campanella* (edibility unknown) has a hairy, chestnut brown to rusty brown cap and stalk; it grows on decaying conifer twigs. *Crinipellis stipitaria* (edibility unknown) has a lighter cap with a dark brown nipple in the center; it grows on lawns and rotting wood. *C. setipes* (inedible) has a wiry stalk and a pale cap with a dark brown center; it occurs scattered (often in large numbers) on decaying hardwood leaves and debris.

Mycena fuliginaria   EDIBILITY UNKNOWN

Cap: 1–3 cm wide; convex to nearly flat with age; cap edge incurved; smooth; grayish brown with blackish brown areas. Flesh thin or thick, firm, white, becoming purple-black where injured. **Gills:** Attached to the stalk, pulling away in older specimens, closely spaced; white, turning black when injured. **Stalk:** 2–5 cm long, 1–2.5 mm thick, equal in thickness overall; smooth or slightly roughened; grayish brown, aging to blackish. **Spore Print:** White. **Fruiting:** Scattered or in groups on decayed wood, mostly hemlock; summer, fall. **Range:** Eastern N. America. **Family:** Tricholomataceae. **Comments:** Formerly known as *Collybia succosa.* The juice of this mushroom turns black upon exposure to air. **Similar Species:** *Mycena taxodii* (edibility unknown) has a conical to convex, grayish brown to black cap with short radial lines near the cap edge, and grayish gills that bruise black; it grows on trunks of cypress.

Entoloma cetratum   EDIBILITY UNKNOWN

Cap: 2–4 cm wide; bell-shaped to convex with age; yellow-brown, darker reddish brown near the center; smooth; with radial lines visible extending from the center to the cap edge when moist; cap edge incurved in young specimens. Flesh thin, soft, pinkish white. **Gills:** Attached to the stalk, somewhat separated; with numerous partial gills; pinkish brown to pinkish white. **Stalk:** 4–8 cm long, 1–2.5 mm thick, nearly equal in thickness overall; silky; white when young, aging to pinkish brown. **Spore Print:** Salmon pink. **Fruiting:** Solitary or scattered among mosses in wet conifer and mixed woods, especially with spruce and hemlock; summer, fall. **Range:** Eastern N. America. **Family:** Entolomataceae. **Comments:** Also known as *Nolanea cetratum.* This mushroom may be more widely distributed than records indicate. **Similar Species:** *Entoloma staurosporum* (edibility unknown) has a conical, grayish brown to yellow-brown cap, short lines visible at the cap edge when moist, and pinkish gills; it grows on grass and in mixed woods.

▲ Zoned-cap Collybia, *Crinipellis zonata*

▲ *Mycena fuliginaria*

▲ *Entoloma cetratum*

SMALL FRAGILE MUSHROOMS

Yellow Unicorn Entoloma, *Entoloma murraii* EDIBILITY UNKNOWN

Cap: 1–3 cm wide; bell-shaped to conical, with a sharp, pointed knob at the center; smooth, shiny; bright yellow to yellowish orange, fading to pale yellow with age. Flesh thin, pale yellowish. **Gills:** Attached to the stalk, somewhat separated; white to pale yellow or pinkish yellow. **Stalk:** 5–8 cm long, 2–5 mm thick, equal in thickness overall; pale yellow to yellow. **Spore Print:** Salmon pink. **Fruiting:** Solitary or in groups on the ground in moist woodlands, usually among mosses; summer, fall. **Range:** Eastern N. America; also Ariz. **Family:** Entolomataceae. **Comments:** Also known as *Nolanea murraii*. It is common in sphagnum bogs, often associated with other *Entoloma* species. **Similar Species:** Salmon Unicorn Entoloma (*E. salmoneum*; edibility unknown) is nearly identical in shape and size, but it has a salmon-colored cap. *E. luteum* (edibility unknown) differs by having a grayish yellow to greenish yellow cap and a slightly to strongly bitter taste.

Pink Mycena, *Mycena pura* EDIBLE (caution)

Cap: 2–5 cm wide; bell-shaped to bluntly convex when young, becoming convex to flat with age; smooth, with short lines visible at the cap edge when moist; color variable—lilac gray, purplish, rosy red, yellowish, or white, fading as it dries; with a bluish tint near the center. Flesh thick, pale purple to white; odor and taste radish-like. **Gills:** Attached to the stalk, sometimes notched, closely spaced; with tiny crossveins; purple-lilac to grayish blue, edges white. **Stalk:** 4–10 cm long, 2–6 mm thick, equal in thickness overall or sometimes enlarged near the base; occasionally twisted; smooth or slightly roughened; slightly paler in color than the cap. **Spore Print:** White. **Fruiting:** Scattered or in groups on the ground in conifer and hardwood forests; spring, summer, fall. **Range:** Throughout N. America. **Family:** Tricholomataceae. **Comments:** Although listed as edible, this mushroom is reported to contain traces of muscarine, a toxin that affects the nervous system. **Similar Species:** *M. abramsii* (edibility unknown) has a broadly conical, grayish brown cap with short lines visible at the cap edge when moist; it lacks the radish-like odor and taste.

Orange Mycena, *Mycena leaiana* EDIBILITY UNKNOWN

Cap: 1–4 cm wide; convex to bell-shaped; smooth, shiny, sticky; bright orange to reddish orange, fading to yellowish orange with age or upon drying. Flesh soft, watery, white. **Gills:** Attached to the stalk, closely spaced; pinkish orange with reddish orange edges. **Stalk:** 3–7 cm long, 2–4 mm thick; sticky, smooth; yellowish orange to orange; covered with dense, pale yellow to yellowish orange hairs at the base. **Spore Print:** White. **Fruiting:** Solitary or clustered on hardwoods, especially beech; summer, fall. **Range:** Northeastern N. America. **Family:** Tricholomataceae. **Comments:** The bright orange cap and reddish-orange gill edges are characteristic. **Similar species:** Red-Orange Mycena (*M. strobilinoides*; edibility unknown) has a conical to bell-shaped, reddish orange cap; it grows on the ground under conifers at higher elevations. *M. atkinsoniana* (edibility unknown) has a reddish orange to reddish brown cap, dull yellow gills with maroon-red edges, and a yellowish brown to purple-brown stalk; it exudes an orange-yellow juice when cut and grows in groups on decaying leaves.

◀ Yellow Unicorn Entoloma
Entoloma murraii

▲ Pink Mycena
Mycena pura

▼ Orange Mycena
Mycena leaiana

SMALL FRAGILE MUSHROOMS

Mycena lilacifolia   INEDIBLE

Cap: 8–25 mm wide; convex to nearly flat; smooth, sticky, with translucent lines at the cap edge; lilac, quickly aging to yellow and becoming paler toward the cap edge. Flesh thin, pale yellow. **Gills:** Attached to and slightly descending the stalk, somewhat separated; lilac, remaining so or slowly becoming more pallid with age. **Stalk:** 1–4.5 cm long, 1–2.5 mm thick, equal in thickness overall; smooth, sticky; lilac when young, aging to yellow; with lilac hairs at the base; interior hollow. **Spore Print:** White. **Fruiting:** Scattered or in groups on conifer logs; spring, summer, fall. **Range:** Northern N. America and at higher elevations in the South. **Family:** Tricholomataceae. **Comments:** This species appears to prefer cold temperatures for fruiting. **Similar Species:** Lavender Baeospora (*Baeospora myriadophylla*; edibility unknown) fades with age from lavender to yellow-brown to pale tannish cream; it never becomes yellow.

Mycena amabilissima   EDIBILITY UNKNOWN

Cap: 3–20 mm wide; conical, becoming bell-shaped with age; edge upturned in some specimens; smooth, slippery; pale coral red, fading to white; translucent, with radial lines near the cap edge. Flesh thin, delicate, white to pinkish white. **Gills:** Attached to the stalk, often with a fine tooth partially descending the stalk; somewhat separated to widely spaced; white to pale pinkish white. **Stalk:** 3–5 cm long, 1–2 mm thick, equal in thickness overall; fragile, watery; white to pale pinkish white; interior hollow. **Spore Print:** White. **Fruiting:** Scattered or in groups in sphagnum moss or on the ground under conifers; spring, summer, fall. **Range:** Widely distributed in N. America. **Family:** Tricholomataceae. **Comments:** This mushroom is common in bogs, particularly in the fall after heavy rains. Little is known regarding the edibility of *Mycena* species. **Similar Species:** Several additional species and varieties, including *M. roseocandida, M. monticola* and *M. subincarnata* (all of unknown edibility), are nearly identical and require microscopic examination for identification.

Walnut Mycena, *Mycena luteopallens*   INEDIBLE

Cap: 1–1.5 cm wide; egg-shaped, becoming broadly conical to bell-shaped and finally convex to flat with age, often with a small central knob; smooth; with translucent lines at the cap edge; orange to yellow, fading with age to pale yellow. Flesh thin, pallid to yellow. **Gills:** Attached to the stalk, widely spaced; yellow to pinkish-tinged, edges paler. **Stalk:** 5–10 cm long, 1–1.5 mm thick; equal in thickness overall; smooth; orange to yellow-orange near the apex, yellow to paler below; interior hollow. **Spore Print:** White. **Fruiting:** Scattered on the usually buried remains of nuts of hickory and walnut; summer, fall. **Range:** Eastern N. America. **Family:** Tricholomataceae. **Comments:** Since the substrate (material on which the mushroom grows) is sometimes buried, care must be used to be sure that the entire mushroom and substrate are collected. **Similar Species:** None. Once seen, it is easy to recognize because of its shape and the distinct substrate association.

◄ *Mycena lilacifolia*

▼ *Mycena amabilissima*

Walnut Mycena ▶
Mycena luteopallens

SMALL FRAGILE MUSHROOMS

Orange Pinwheel Marasmius, *Marasmius siccus*
EDIBILITY UNKNOWN

Cap: 5–30 mm wide; convex to bell-shaped; often depressed in the center or with a small knob; deeply grooved; felt-like to nearly smooth; rusty orange. Flesh thin, whitish or pale yellow. **Gills:** Attached to the stalk, becoming free in older specimens; widely spaced; white to pale yellow. **Stalk:** 2–8 cm long, 0.2–1 mm thick, equal in thickness overall; straight; smooth; white or yellowish white above, reddish brown below. **Spore Print:** White. **Fruiting:** Scattered or in groups on leaves, pine needles, and wood; summer, fall. **Range:** Eastern N. America. **Family:** Tricholomataceae. **Comments:** Several species are nearly identical but have slightly different colors. Microscopic examination is needed to identify these species. **Similar Species:** Pinwheel Marasmius (*M. rotula*; edibility unknown) has a bell-shaped, deeply grooved, white cap and grows in dense clusters on rotting wood. Garlic Marasmius (*M. scorodonius*; edible) has a slightly wrinkled, reddish brown to pinkish tan cap and a garlic odor and taste; it grows on fallen twigs and woody debris. *M. fulvoferrugineus* (edibility unknown) has a dark rusty brown cap, and *M. pulcherripes* (edibility unknown) has a pinkish (aging to yellowish brown) cap; both grow on hardwood leaf litter.

Pleated Marasmius, *Marasmius plicatulus*   EDIBILITY UNKNOWN

Cap: 1–4 cm wide; conical to convex; pleated-wrinkled at the cap edge in mature specimens; velvety, often with a frosted sheen; dark wine red, maroon, or bay brown, sometimes paler at the edge. Flesh thin, tough, white. **Gills:** Almost free of the stalk, widely spaced; white to tinged slightly pinkish. **Stalk:** 6–13 cm long, 1.5–3.5 mm thick; rigid and brittle; smooth, shiny; pallid above, reddish brown to reddish black below. **Spore Print:** White. **Fruiting:** Solitary, scattered, or in small groups under conifers and hardwoods; fall, winter. **Range:** Pacific Northwest. **Family:** Tricholomataceae. **Comments:** The velvety cap and deep rich color make this a most beautiful species. **Similar Species:** *M. sullivantii* (edibility unknown) is smaller, and its rich orange-red to red cap lacks the wine red tints; it occurs in eastern N. America.

Marasmius delectans   EDIBILITY UNKNOWN

Cap: 5–40 mm wide; convex to nearly flat with age; with an upturned, wavy edge in older specimens; dry, smooth, becoming wrinkled; cream to white, darker near the center. Flesh moderately thick, white to pale yellow; odor mild to somewhat foul. **Gills:** Attached to the stalk, sometimes with a notch, or free of the stalk in older specimens; somewhat separated to widely spaced; cream to white. **Stalk:** 1–7.5 cm long, 1–3.5 mm thick, equal in thickness overall; dry, shiny, smooth; yellowish white, aging to grayish brown; interior hollow. **Spore Print:** White. **Fruiting:** Scattered or clustered on decaying leaves and twigs in hardwood forests; summer, fall. **Range:** Eastern N. America. **Family:** Tricholomataceae. **Comments:** The combination of pale yellowish white cap, hollow grayish brown stalk, and fruiting on leaves and twigs is characteristic. **Similar Species:** *M. spissus* (edibility unknown) has a smooth, yellowish brown to pinkish brown cap, closely spaced gills, and a stalk that is yellowish brown near the top and chestnut brown below; it grows on hardwood leaf litter.

▲ Orange Pinwheel Marasmius
Marasmius siccus

Pleated Marasmius ▶
Marasmius plicatulus

▼ *Marasmius delectans*

SMALL FRAGILE MUSHROOMS

Marasmius glabellus   EDIBILITY UNKNOWN

Cap: 5–25 mm wide; convex or bell-shaped when young, aging to nearly flat; sometimes with a low knob or depression at the center; dry, smooth, sometimes with shallow grooves; yellowish brown. Flesh thin, yellowish white. **Gills:** Attached to the stalk, becoming free in older specimens; widely spaced, with crossveins in older specimens; white to pale yellow. **Stalk:** 1.5–6 cm long, 1–2 mm thick; nearly equal in thickness overall; centrally attached to the cap; dry, shiny, smooth; white to yellowish near the top, yellowish brown below. **Spore Print:** White. **Fruiting:** Scattered or in groups on decaying leaves in hardwood forests; summer, early fall. **Range:** Eastern N. America. **Family:** Tricholomataceae. **Comments:** The combination of yellowish brown cap and widely spaced gills is characteristic. **Similar Species:** M. *sullivantii* (edibility unknown) has a bright orange to reddish orange cap, closely spaced gills, and white hairs at the base of the stalk; it grows on decaying leaves, wood, and debris.

Black-footed Marasmius, *Marasmiellus nigripes*
EDIBILITY UNKNOWN

Cap: 1–2 cm wide; convex to nearly flat with age; thin, wrinkled, dry, powdery; white. Flesh thin, firm to rubbery, white. **Gills:** Attached to and sometimes partially descending the stalk, widely spaced; with crossveins; white, bruising pinkish red where injured. **Stalk:** 2–5 cm long, 1–1.5 mm thick, tapering slightly toward the base; black; covered with tiny white hairs that give the surface a granular appearance. **Spore Print:** White. **Fruiting:** Scattered or in groups on decaying leaves and twigs in mixed woods; fall. **Range:** Eastern N. America. **Family:** Tricholomataceae. **Comments:** Formerly known as *Heliomyces nigripes.* This mushroom has unusual, triangular to star-like spores. **Similar Species:** White Marasmius (*Marasmiellus albuscorticis*; edibility unknown) has a small white stalk and grows on decaying stems and twigs.

Xeromphalina cauticinalis   EDIBILITY UNKNOWN

Cap: 5–25 mm wide; convex to nearly flat with age; smooth, with short radial lines near the cap edge; golden yellow. Flesh thin, flexible, pale yellow; turning red in 3% solution of potassium hydroxide. **Gills:** Partially descending the stalk, somewhat separated; with crossveins; pale yellow. **Stalk:** 3–8 cm long, 1–2.5 mm thick, equal in thickness overall; sparsely covered with very short hairs; yellow-brown, becoming dark brown toward the base. **Spore Print:** White. **Fruiting:** Solitary to scattered or in groups on conifer debris or decaying poplar leaves; summer, fall. **Range:** Widely distributed in N. America. **Family:** Tricholomataceae. **Comments:** The stalks tend to be straight. **Similar Species:** Fuzzy Foot (*X. campanella*; edibility unknown) grows on decaying conifer logs and stumps. Kauffman's Xeromphalina (*X. kauffmanii*; edibility unknown) grows on decaying hardwood logs and stumps. Both have an orange-brown cap with a depressed center and a curved stalk with dark brown hairs on the lower portion.

▲ Marasmius glabellus

▲ Black-footed Marasmius, Marasmiellus nigripes

▼ Xeromphalina cauticinalis

SMALL FRAGILE MUSHROOMS

Haymaker's Mushroom, *Panaeolus foenisecii*
POISONOUS (hallucinogenic)

Cap: 5–30 mm wide; convex to bell-shaped; reddish brown to grayish brown; dry; with short lines visible at the cap edge when moist. Flesh thin, water-soaked, grayish brown to tan. **Gills:** Attached to the stalk, closely spaced; purple-brown to dark brownish black. **Stalk:** 2.5–10 cm long, 1.5–3 mm thick, equal in thickness overall or slightly enlarged near the base; white to pinkish brown. **Spore Print:** Purple-brown. **Fruiting:** Scattered on lawns and in grassy areas; spring through fall. **Range:** Widely distributed in N. America. **Family:** Coprinaceae. **Comments:** Low levels of hallucinogenic compounds have been reported in this species. The mushrooms are fresh in morning dew but often wilt in the hot sun. **Similar Species:** Bell-cap Panaeolus (*P. campanulatus*; edibility unknown) has a bell-shaped, brownish cap; a long, fuzzy, brownish gray stalk; and tooth-like white tissue hanging on the cap edge. Girdled Panaeolus (*P. subbalteatus*; poisonous, hallucinogenic) has a reddish brown cap with a darker circular zone near the edge; it grows on lawns, in gardens, and on other manured soil.

Conocybe subovalis   EDIBILITY UNKNOWN

Cap: 5–35 mm wide; oval to bell-shaped when young, becoming convex or bell-shaped with age; smooth, shiny; yellowish brown to reddish brown; with radial lines visible extending from the center to the cap edge when moist. Flesh thin, soft, water-soaked, yellowish brown. **Gills:** Attached to the stalk, becoming nearly free with age; closely spaced; pale yellow to reddish brown. **Stalk:** 6–14 cm long, 1–4 mm thick, abruptly bulbous at the base; reddish brown, often developing whitish areas near the base in mature specimens. **Spore Print:** Reddish brown. **Fruiting:** Solitary or in groups on manured lawns, in gardens, and on dung piles; summer, fall. **Range:** Eastern N. America. **Family:** Bolbitiaceae. **Comments:** Probably more widely distributed than reports indicate. **Similar Species:** Brown Dunce Cap (*C. tenera*; edibility unknown) has a conical, yellow-brown cap, cinnamon brown gills, and a pale brown stalk up to 8.5 cm long; it grows on lawns. Dunce Cap (*C. lactea*; edibility unknown) has a conical, dull white cap, a dull white stalk, and cinnamon gills; it also grows on lawns.

Collybia cookei   INEDIBLE

Cap: 2–7 mm wide; convex, becoming flat with age; edge incurved to inrolled when young; smooth; white to pinkish buff, fading to dull white. Flesh thin, white. **Gills:** Attached to the stalk, closely spaced; white to pinkish buff. **Stalk:** 4–50 mm long, 1–2 mm thick, equal in thickness overall; fibrous, hairy near the base; pale cinnamon to somewhat darker; arising from a small (up to 10 × 8 mm), wrinkled, nut-like, dull yellow to pale tan mass (sclerotium). **Spore Print:** White. **Fruiting:** In groups on old, blackened mushroom remains or in rich humus in conifer and hardwood forests; summer, fall. **Range:** Widely distributed throughout N. America. **Family:** Tricholomataceae. **Comments:** This is one of several species of similar stature and color that often occur on the same substrate—old, blackened mushroom remains. Each must be excavated carefully to obtain the associated sclerotium (when present). **Similar Species:** Tuberous Collybia (*C. tuberosa*; inedible) is attached to an elongated, reddish brown, seed-like sclerotium. *C. cirrhata* (inedible) does not form a sclerotium.

▲ Haymaker's Mushroom
Panaeolus foenisecii

▼ *Collybia cookei*

◄ *Conocybe subovalis*

BRITTLE MUSHROOMS

WITH LATEX

Hygrophorus Milky, *Lactarius hygrophoroides*   EDIBLE, choice

Cap: 3–10 cm wide; convex to nearly flat, sometimes depressed in the center; cap edge inrolled in young specimens; dry, smooth to slightly velvety; orange-brown or dull cinnamon. Flesh thick, firm, white. **Gills:** Attached to and partially descending the stalk, widely spaced; white, aging to cream-colored or yellowish brown; with tiny crossveins. Latex white. **Stalk:** 3–5 cm long, 5–15 mm thick, nearly equal in thickness overall; dry; coloration like the cap's or somewhat lighter; interior solid. **Spore Print:** White. **Fruiting:** Solitary or scattered on soil; summer, early fall. **Range:** Eastern N. America, west to Mich. and Ariz. **Family:** Russulaceae. **Comments:** The latex does not change color over time, and the tissues show no color change when injured. **Similar Species:** Voluminous-latex Milky (*L. volemus*; edible, choice) has a smooth cap. Corrugated-cap Milky (*L. corrugis*; edible, choice) has a reddish brown cap with corrugations principally at the edge. Both have closely spaced gills, a white latex that slowly turns brown and stains tissues brown, and a somewhat fish-like odor.

Indigo Milky, *Lactarius indigo*   EDIBLE

Cap: 5–15 cm wide; convex to slightly depressed (becoming sunken in some specimens); cap edge inrolled in young specimens; smooth, sticky; with concentric zones of dark blue to grayish blue; greenish blue where bruised. Flesh thick, firm, white, quickly turning blue when injured. **Gills:** Attached to the stalk, closely spaced; blue, becoming yellowish blue with age, slowly turning green when bruised. Latex blue, slowly turning dark green. **Stalk:** 2–8 cm long, 1–2.5 cm thick, nearly equal in thickness overall; dark blue to silvery blue. **Spore Print:** Cream yellow. **Fruiting:** Scattered or in groups on the ground; summer, fall. **Range:** Eastern N. America, west to Mich. and Ariz. **Family:** Russulaceae. **Comments:** This mushroom is easy to recognize because of its dark blue color and blue latex. **Similar Species:** Silver-Blue Milky (*L. paradoxus*; edible) has a grayish blue cap and produces a wine brown latex.

Variegated Milky, *Lactarius subpurpureus*   EDIBLE

Cap: 3–10 cm wide; convex to depressed or nearly flat with age; smooth; wine red, zoned with lighter pink, sometimes spotted with emerald green. Flesh white to pink, staining red then slowly green when injured; taste mild to slightly bitter. **Gills:** Attached to and sometimes partially descending the stalk, somewhat separated; with coloration like the cap's, becoming green-spotted with age. Latex wine red, scanty, mild to slightly peppery. **Stalk:** 3–8 cm long, 6–15 mm thick, nearly equal in thickness overall; of the same color as the cap, aging darker, with dull red spots. **Spore Print:** Cream yellow. **Fruiting:** Scattered on the soil under conifers and in mixed woods; summer, fall. **Range:** Eastern N. America, south to Tenn. and N.C. **Family:** Russulaceae. **Comments:** This mushroom often fruits in large numbers during periods of high humidity. **Similar Species:** Silver-Blue Milky (*L. paradoxus*; edible) has more closely spaced gills and a grayish blue cap; it produces a wine brown latex.

▲ Hygrophorus Milky, *Lactarius hygrophoroides*

▲ Indigo Milky, *Lactarius indigo*

▼ Variegated Milky, *Lactarius subpurpureus*

BRITTLE MUSHROOMS

WITH LATEX

Common Violet-latex Milky, *Lactarius uvidus* POISONOUS

Cap: 3–10 cm wide; convex to nearly flat, becoming slightly depressed with age; smooth, sticky; pale lilac to slightly darker, typically lacking color zones. Flesh thick, firm, white, staining purple when injured; taste bitter to slightly hot. **Gills:** Attached to or partly descending the stalk, closely spaced; creamy white, bruising purple when injured. Latex white, staining tissues purple. **Stalk:** 3–7 cm long, 1–1.5 cm thick, equal in thickness overall; slimy; white to pale lilac, often yellowish near the base. **Spore Print:** Pale yellow. **Fruiting:** Scattered or in groups on the ground and among mosses in mixed woods; summer, fall. **Range:** Northern N. America and at higher elevations in the South. **Family:** Russulaceae. **Comments:** One of several species with white latex that stains tissues purple to lilac. **Similar Species:** *L. subpalustris* (edibility unknown) has a larger (10–20 cm wide), dull gray cap with tawny olive spots. *L. maculatus* (edibility unknown) has a zoned, grayish brown to pale lilac cap; its flesh tastes very hot. Both have watery white latex that stains tissues purple.

Lactarius xanthogalactus EDIBILITY UNKNOWN

Cap: 2–10 cm wide; convex, becoming flat to uplifted with age, with a depressed center; smooth; somewhat sticky; pinkish orange, becoming reddish brown to brownish orange with age; with obscure zones. Flesh thick, brittle, white to pale orange, rapidly turning yellow when exposed; taste slowly perceived as peppery (acrid). **Gills:** Attached to the stalk, closely spaced to somewhat separated; cream, pale orange, or salmon; when cut or broken, exuding a white latex that rapidly turns bright yellow. **Stalk:** 2–10 cm long, 7–20 mm thick, equal in thickness overall; pale orange to salmon to grayish red; flesh white to light orange, rapidly turning yellow when exposed; interior hollow. **Spore Print:** Cream. **Fruiting:** Scattered or in groups in mixed forests; late summer, fall (also early winter in Calif.). **Range:** Western N. America. **Family:** Russulaceae. **Comments:** One of several *Lactarius* species with white latex that rapidly turns yellow. **Similar Species:** Yellow-latex Milky (*L. vinaceorufescens*; possibly poisonous), a northeastern species, is very similar (and may in fact be the same species). *L. chrysorheus* (possibly poisonous) is a pallid to pinkish yellow eastern species that appears more common in the South. Both have white latex that turns yellow.

Orange-latex Milky, *Lactarius deliciosus* EDIBLE

Cap: 2–13 cm wide; broadly convex to nearly flat with age; smooth, slippery when wet; carrot orange, with several concentric rings of paler orange, becoming green-spotted with age. Flesh yellowish orange, bruising greenish; taste mild; odor fruity. **Gills:** Attached to and sometimes partially descending the stalk, closely spaced. Latex orange, slowly staining tissues green. **Stalk:** 4–7.5 cm long, 1.5–3 cm thick, slightly narrowing at the base; smooth, dry; orange, developing green spots with age. **Spore Print:** Yellowish white. **Fruiting:** Solitary, scattered, or in loosely clustered groups on the ground under conifers; late summer, fall, winter. **Range:** Throughout N. America. **Family:** Russulaceae. **Comments:** Although edible, it is not as tasty as its name implies. **Similar Species:** *L. thyinos* (edible) has a sticky stalk and does not develop green stains; it grows in northern wetlands. *L. rubrilacteus* (edible) displays a scant, reddish latex.

▲ Common Violet-latex Milky, *Lactarius uvidus*

◄ *Lactarius xanthogalactus*

▼ Orange-latex Milky, *Lactarius deliciosus*

BRITTLE MUSHROOMS

WITH LATEX

Peppery Milky, *Lactarius piperatus*   EDIBLE (caution)

Cap: 5–15 cm wide; convex, becoming flat to somewhat depressed with age; dry; white to creamy white with age. Flesh thick, firm, white; odor absent or slightly disagreeable; taste very quickly perceived as hot. **Gills:** Attached to the stalk, crowded together, often forking; white to pale cream yellow. Latex white; taste very quickly perceived as hot. **Stalk:** 2–8 cm long, 1–2.5 cm thick, nearly equal in thickness overall; dry; white; interior solid. **Spore Print:** White. **Fruiting:** Scattered on the ground in hardwood forests; summer, fall. **Range:** Eastern N. America, west to Mich. **Family:** Russulaceae. **Comments:** This mushroom is very hot in taste and must be parboiled before it can be eaten. **Similar Species:** *L. piperatus* var. *glaucescens* (poisonous) has latex that dries pale green. Deceptive Milky (*L. deceptivus*; edibility unknown) has more widely spaced gills and a cottony, inrolled cap edge, especially in younger specimens. *L. vellereus* (edibility unknown) and *L. subvellereus* (edible) both have gills that range from crowded to widely spaced and exude an off-white to pale cream latex. These two species and *L. piperatus* can be distinguished only by means of fine microscopic features.

WITHOUT LATEX

Short-stalked White Russula, *Russula brevipes*   EDIBLE (caution)

Cap: 8–20 cm wide; convex, becoming nearly flat or usually somewhat depressed with age; cap edge inrolled; dry; white to cream white, developing dull brown discolorations with age. Flesh thick, firm, brittle, white. **Gills:** Attached to and partially descending the stalk; closely spaced to crowded together; white, developing dull brown or yellowish discolorations with age. **Stalk:** 2–7.5 cm long, 2–4 cm thick, nearly equal in thickness overall; white, bruising brown when handled. **Spore Print:** Pale creamy white. **Fruiting:** Scattered on the ground in mixed woods; summer, fall. **Range:** Widely distributed in N. America. **Family:** Russulaceae. **Comments:** Formerly known as *R. delica*. Edible only if specially prepared. When parasitized by the Lobster Fungus (*Hypomyces lactifluorum*), however, it becomes an excellent edible and needs no special preparation. **Similar Species:** Peppery Milky (*Lactarius piperatus*; edible) has crowded gills and white latex. *Lactarius vellereus* (edibility unknown) has widely spaced gills and white latex.

Firm Russula, *Russula compacta*   EDIBLE

Cap: 5–20 cm wide; convex, aging to nearly flat, with a depressed center; cap edge inrolled in young specimens; slimy when fresh; white, aging to yellow-brown in the center of the cap. Flesh thick, firm, brittle, white; odor fish-like in older specimens. **Gills:** Attached to or partially descending the stalk, closely spaced to crowded together; white, bruising or aging to dull cinnamon brown. **Stalk:** 3–12 cm long, 1–4 cm thick, nearly equal in thickness overall or tapering toward the base; white. **Spore Print:** White. **Fruiting:** Scattered or in groups on the ground and among mosses in wet woodlands; summer, fall. **Range:** Widely distributed in N. America. **Family:** Russulaceae. **Comments:** This mushroom is often abundant in wet lowlands, especially near bogs. **Similar Species:** Graying Yellow Russula (*R. claroflava*; edible) has a yellow cap with white gills and stalk; the cap flesh and stalk bruise ash gray when injured.

▲ Peppery Milky
Lactarius piperatus

▲ Short-stalked White Russula, *Russula brevipes*

▼ Firm Russula, *Russula compacta*

BRITTLE MUSHROOMS

WITHOUT LATEX

Emetic Russula, *Russula emetica*   POISONOUS

Cap: 2.5–7.5 cm wide; convex to flat with age, somewhat depressed near the center in most specimens; sticky; bright red or deep pink. Flesh thick, brittle, white; odor absent; taste very quickly perceived as hot. **Gills:** Attached to the stalk, closely spaced; white to creamy white. **Stalk:** 5–10 cm long, 5–25 mm thick, enlarging slightly toward the base; dry; white. **Spore Print:** White. **Fruiting:** Solitary or in groups in sphagnum moss near bogs. **Range:** Widely distributed in N. America; summer, fall. **Family:** Russulaceae. **Comments:** This mushroom is known to cause nausea and vomiting, hence the species name *emetica*. **Similar Species:** *R. silvicola* (edibility unknown) is similar in appearance but grows in drier mixed woodlands. Several other red species are also common in dry woodlands; all are best identified with a microscope.

Almond-scented Russula, *Russula laurocerasi*   INEDIBLE

Cap: 2.5–12.5 cm wide; convex to nearly flat with age, usually somewhat depressed; cap edge incurved in young specimens; slimy and shiny when wet; yellowish brown to yellowish tan; with rough, shallow grooves near the edge. Flesh thick, firm, brittle, pale yellow; odor of almond extract, sometimes becoming fetid; taste unpleasant. **Gills:** Attached to the stalk, closely to widely spaced; cream white. **Stalk:** 2.5–10 cm long, 1–3 cm thick, nearly equal in thickness overall; smooth; yellowish white. **Spore Print:** Yellow-orange. **Fruiting:** Scattered or in groups on the soil in mixed woods; summer, fall. **Range:** Widely distributed in N. America. **Family:** Russulaceae. **Comments:** This species is inedible because of its fetid odor and disagreeable taste. **Similar Species:** *R. fragrantissima* (inedible) has a larger, darker cap and a fetid odor. *R. granulata* (edibility unknown) also has an almond-like odor but exhibits crust-like scales near the cap center.

Russula pulverulenta   EDIBILITY UNKNOWN

Cap: 3.5–8 cm wide; nearly round when young, becoming convex to nearly flat or somewhat funnel-shaped with age; sticky when wet; dark grayish yellow to yellowish brown, paler with age; covered with thin, cottony, pale yellow scales (most obvious at the center). Flesh thick, brittle, yellowish white. **Gills:** Attached to the stalk, closely spaced to somewhat separated; with small crossveins; brittle; white, aging to pale yellowish, sometimes brown-spotted. **Stalk:** 3–5.5 cm long, 8–20 mm thick, equal in thickness overall or enlarging below; yellowish white above, light yellow below, developing brownish spots with age; with thin, cottony scales (like those on the cap) at the base; interior stuffed, mealy-granular. **Spore Print:** Pale orange-yellow. **Fruiting:** Solitary, scattered, or in groups in soil under conifers and hardwoods; summer, fall. **Range:** Eastern N. America. **Family:** Russulaceae. **Comments:** The yellow scales, called floccules, are most obvious in fresh, young specimens. **Similar Species:** *R. pectinatoides* (edibility unknown) has a somewhat darker cap and lacks the thin yellow scales.

▲ Emetic Russula, *Russula emetica*

▲ Almond-scented Russula, *Russula laurocerasi*

▼ *Russula pulverulenta*

OTHER MUSHROOMS WITH DESCENDING GILLS

Jack O'Lantern, *Omphalotus olearius*   POISONOUS

Cap: 5–18 cm wide; broadly convex to nearly flat, becoming depressed in the center; smooth; yellow-orange to orange. Flesh yellow; taste mild; odor disagreeable. **Gills:** Descending the stalk, closely spaced. **Stalk:** 5–20 cm long, 9–20 mm thick, becoming narrow and often fused with others near the base; pale yellow to pale orange, sometimes vertically streaked; interior not hollow. **Spore Print:** Pale cream. **Fruiting:** In clusters on hardwood stumps and buried wood; late summer, fall. **Range:** Widespread in eastern N. America, west to Ariz. **Family:** Tricholomataceae. **Comments:** Formerly known as *Clitocybe illudens*. This mushroom causes strong gastrointestinal upset. The common name refers to the bioluminescent gills—when fresh, they glow in the dark. As a result, it is one of several species known as "ghosts of the forest." **Similar Species:** Chanterelle (*Cantharellus cibarius;* edible) has thick, blunt, shallow, widely spaced gills and grows on the ground—usually not in clusters.

Western Jack O'Lantern, *Omphalotus olivascens*   POISONOUS

Cap: 4–24 cm wide; broadly convex, aging to flat; edge decurved when young, becoming uplifted; smooth; dull reddish orange to brownish orange, tinged with olive in older specimens. Flesh thin except at the center, with coloration like the cap's. **Gills:** Descending the stalk, closely spaced; yellowish orange, becoming olive-tinged. **Stalk:** 4–22 cm long, 7–80 mm thick, tapering and often fused at the base; smooth; with coloration like the cap's, often vertically streaked; interior solid. **Spore Print:** White. **Fruiting:** Solitary (rarely) or clustered on stumps and buried wood of hardwoods; fall, winter. **Range:** Ore. and Calif. **Family:** Tricholomataceae. **Comments:** As with the eastern Jack O'Lantern, this species causes gastrointestinal distress and has gills that glow in the dark. **Similar Species:** The eastern Jack O'Lantern (*O. olearius;* poisonous) is brighter and lacks the more somber olive tones.

Ringless Honey Mushroom, *Armillariella tabescens*   EDIBLE (caution)

Cap: 2.5–10 cm wide; convex, becoming flat, then depressed with age; smooth or with scant, scattered hairs and scales (especially in the center); pinkish brown to yellowish brown to dull rusty brown. Flesh thick at the center, thinner elsewhere, white. **Gills:** Descending the stalk, closely spaced; white, becoming pinkish white or darker with age. **Stalk:** 7.5–20 cm long, 5–15 mm thick, tapered toward the base; with scattered, longitudinal fibers and small scales; dull white to streaked with olive-tan; interior stuffed to hollow. **Spore Print:** White. **Fruiting:** In clusters (often large ones) at the bases of trees and stumps or on buried hardwood; late summer, fall. **Range:** Eastern N. America. **Family:** Tricholomataceae. **Comments:** Also known as *Armillaria tabescens*. Although considered edible, this species causes gastrointestinal distress in some people. **Similar Species:** Honey Mushroom (*Armillariella mellea;* edible) has a sticky to slippery cap (in fresh specimens) and a ring on the stalk; it tends to fruit later and in smaller clusters. The eastern Jack O'Lantern (*Omphalotus olearius;* poisonous) also grows in clusters but is larger; its cap color exhibits intense orange tones, and its gills descend the stalk to a greater extent.

▲ Jack O'Lantern, *Omphalotus olearius*

▲ Western Jack O'Lantern
Omphalotus olivascens

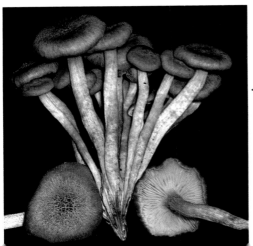

◀ Ringless Honey
Mushroom
*Armillariella
tabescens*

OTHER MUSHROOMS WITH DESCENDING GILLS

Poison Paxillus, *Paxillus involutus* POISONOUS

Cap: 5–12 cm wide; convex to flat with age, somewhat depressed in the center; dry to slimy when wet; yellow-brown to reddish brown. Flesh thick, firm, pale yellowish brown, bruising darker brown. **Gills:** Descending the stalk, crowded together; yellowish brown, turning dark brown where injured. **Stalk:** 4–10 cm long, 1–2 cm thick; equal in thickness overall to slightly enlarged at the base; yellowish brown with dark brown streaks. **Spore Print:** Brown. **Fruiting:** Solitary or in groups on the ground in conifer and hardwood forests and gardens with shrubs; summer, fall. **Range:** Widely distributed in N. America. **Family:** Paxillaceae. **Comments:** There are conflicting reports regarding the edibility of this mushroom; because of reports of poisonings, we have listed it as a poisonous species. **Similar Species:** Velvet-footed Pax (*P. atrotomentosus;* inedible) has a hairy, brownish black stalk. False Chanterelle (*Hygrophoropsis aurantiaca;* edible, caution) has a brownish orange to yellowish orange cap and forked gills; it grows on the ground or on rotting wood.

White Leucopax, *Leucopaxillus albissimus* INEDIBLE

Cap: 2.5–10 cm wide; convex to nearly flat with age; with an incurved edge in young specimens; smooth, dry; white. Flesh thick, firm, white; odor somewhat fragrant; taste bitter. **Gills:** Attached to and sometimes partially descending the stalk, crowded together; white. **Stalk:** 5–8 cm long, 5–15 mm thick; base bulbous; smooth; white; with a dense, white, cottony net at the point of attachment. **Spore Print:** White. **Fruiting:** Solitary or scattered on the ground in conifer forests; summer, fall. **Range:** Widely distributed in N. America. **Family:** Tricholomataceae. **Comments:** This mushroom is reportedly edible, but most who try it state that it is unpalatable and difficult to digest. **Similar Species:** Bitter Leucopax (*L. amarus;* inedible) has a reddish brown cap and a chalk white stalk with a base covered with dense, white hairs; its flesh has a bitter taste.

Aborted Entoloma, *Entoloma abortivum* EDIBLE (caution)

Cap: 4–10 cm wide; convex to nearly flat with age; edge inrolled, especially in younger specimens; smooth to somewhat roughened with fine hairs; grayish brown. Flesh soft, moderately thick, white; odor and taste farinaceous (metallic-mealy). **Gills:** Descending the stalk, closely spaced; pale gray, aging to salmon pink. **Stalk:** 3–10 cm long, 5–15 mm thick, equal in thickness overall or somewhat enlarged near the base; grayish white; interior solid. **Spore Print:** Salmon pink. **Fruiting:** Scattered or in groups on the ground in conifer and hardwood forests; fall. **Range:** Eastern N. America, west to Kan. and Ariz. **Family:** Entolomataceae. **Comments:** This mushroom is often found together with its aborted forms, which are spongy, oval to irregularly shaped fruiting bodies, 3–8 cm wide, white on the outside, white with reddish streaks on the inside. Both forms are edible. If the aborted forms are not present, this mushroom may easily be confused with poisonous Entoloma species. **Similar Species:** Lead Poisoner (*E. sinuatum;* poisonous) has a slippery, shiny, grayish to brownish cap and gills that do not descend the stalk; it exhibits a farinaceous odor.

▲ Poison Paxillus, *Paxillus involutus*

▲ White Leucopax, *Leucopaxillus albissimus*

Aborted Entoloma ▶
Entoloma abortivum

OTHER MUSHROOMS WITH DESCENDING GILLS

False Chanterelle, *Hygrophoropsis aurantiaca*   EDIBLE (caution)

Cap: 2–8 cm wide; convex to nearly flat with age; with an inrolled edge in younger specimens; minutely hairy, especially near the center; brownish orange, fading to yellowish orange, darkest in the center. Flesh thin, firm, white to pale yellowish orange. **Gills:** Descending the stalk, closely spaced; forked; yellow-orange to orange. **Stalk:** 2–10 cm long, 5–15 mm thick, enlarged toward the base; smooth to slightly roughened, dry; orange to brownish orange. **Spore Print:** White. **Fruiting:** Solitary or in groups on rotting wood or on the ground in mixed forests; late summer, fall. **Range:** Widely distributed in N. America. **Family:** Tricholomataceae. **Comments:** This mushroom is listed in some books as *Clitocybe aurantiaca* and was once thought to be poisonous. **Similar Species:** Chanterelle (*Cantharellus cibarius;* edible) is yellow and has thick gill edges; it grows on the ground. In the East, the much larger Jack O'Lantern (*Omphalotus olearius;* poisonous) is bright orange and has sharp-edged gills; it grows in fused clusters on wood.

Funnel Clitocybe, *Clitocybe gibba*   EDIBLE

Cap: 4–8 cm wide; funnel-shaped; smooth, dry, pinkish tan, aging to darker near the center. Flesh thin, soft, white; odor fragrant; taste mild. **Gills:** Descending the stalk, closely spaced; white. **Stalk:** 4–8 cm long, 5–10 mm thick, nearly equal in thickness overall or enlarging somewhat near the base; smooth; dull white. **Spore Print:** White. **Fruiting:** Solitary or scattered on the ground in hardwood and mixed forests; summer, fall (also winter in Calif.). **Range:** Widely distributed in N. America. **Family:** Tricholomataceae. **Comments:** Formerly known as *C. infundibuliformis.* **Similar Species:** *C. phaeophthalma* = *C. hydrogramma* (edibility unknown) has a creamy white cap and stalk and a disagreeable odor. *C. squamulosa* (edibility unknown) has a yellow-brown cap and stalk, white gills, and a mild odor and taste; it grows on the ground under conifers.

Clitocybe subconnexa   EDIBILITY UNKNOWN

Cap: 3–9 cm wide; convex to nearly flat with age; cap edge incurved in young specimens; often with a slight central depression; silky smooth, dry; white, sometimes with pale yellowish brown discolorations, especially near the center. Flesh moderately thick, brittle, white or pinkish; odor fragrant; taste bitter or mild. **Gills:** Attached to and sometimes slightly descending the stalk, crowded together; pale pinkish brown to dull white. **Stalk:** 2.5–8 cm long, 5–12 mm thick, enlarged slightly toward the base; smooth; dull grayish white to pinkish brown. **Spore Print:** Pinkish cinnamon. **Fruiting:** Clustered on the ground under conifers and hardwoods; summer, fall (also winter in the Northwest). **Range:** Widely distributed in N. America. **Family:** Tricholomataceae. **Comments:** Formerly known as *Clitopilus caespitosus.* Clustered growth is an important feature for identifying this mushroom. **Similar Species:** *Clitocybe fasciculata* (edibility unknown) is nearly identical and is best separated by its rancid to mealy odor. *C. densifolia* (edibility unknown) is nearly identical to *C. subconnexa* and also has a fragrant odor; it is distinguished by its smaller spore size.

▲ False Chanterelle
Hygrophoropsis aurantiaca

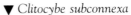

◀ Funnel Clitocybe
Clitocybe gibba

▼ *Clitocybe subconnexa*

OTHER MUSHROOMS WITH DESCENDING GILLS

Clitocybe sclerotoidea   EDIBILITY UNKNOWN

Cap: 8–50 mm wide; convex, becoming flat with age and finally shallowly funnel-shaped, sometimes with a slight knob; edge incurved when young, wavy when mature; pallid to grayish buff or dull tan, with a thin whitish bloom. Flesh thick in the center, white. **Gills:** Attached to the stalk, slightly to moderately descending the stalk, somewhat separated; pale to dark buff, aging to gray or grayish brown. **Stalk:** 2–8 cm long, 3–11 mm thick, equal in thickness overall or tapering above; covered with a layer of fine, short hairs; white to pallid; interior solid; attached to a large (up to 6 × 4 cm), irregular mass (sclerotium). **Spore Print:** White. **Fruiting:** In clusters under pine; late spring, summer, fall. **Range:** Pacific Coast. **Family:** Tricholomataceae. **Comments:** The sclerotium at the base of the mushroom is the parasitized remains of the Fluted Black Helvella (*Helvella lacunosa*; edible, caution). **Similar Species:** *Clitocybe inornata* (edibility unknown) is similar in stature and color but lacks the sclerotium at the base.

Lentinus adhaerens   EDIBILITY UNKNOWN

Cap: 2–8 cm wide; convex to nearly flat with age, sometimes slightly depressed in the center; minutely hairy to nearly smooth, somewhat sticky; creamy white to pinkish orange, with reddish orange spots. Flesh firm, white to yellowish brown. **Gills:** Attached to and partially descending the stalk, somewhat separated; sometimes forked; edges becoming slightly tooth-like; creamy white. **Stalk:** 2–8 cm long, 5–15 mm thick, equal in thickness overall; centrally attached to the cap or sometimes off-center; creamy white to pinkish orange, with reddish orange spots; interior solid. **Spore Print:** White. **Fruiting:** Solitary or in groups on conifer and hardwood stumps and branches; spring. **Range:** Maine and N.H.; probably more widely distributed. **Family:** Tricholomataceae. **Comments:** This mushroom fruits during April when warming temperatures begin to melt the snow. Not commonly collected because of its fruiting season. **Similar Species:** *L. kauffmanii* (edibility unknown) is nearly identical but it lacks the sticky surface and reddish orange spots, and its spores are smaller; it occurs in the Northwest from Alaska south to Calif.

Gray Almond Waxy Cap, *Hygrophorus agathosmus*   EDIBLE

Cap: 2–8 cm wide; convex to nearly flat with age; slimy, sticky, smooth; grayish white to grayish brown, darkest over the center. Flesh soft, white to grayish white; odor of almonds. **Gills:** Attached to and slightly descending the stalk, somewhat separated, occasionally forked; waxy; white. **Stalk:** 5–8 cm long, 5–20 mm thick, nearly equal in thickness overall; smooth, dry; white to grayish white. **Spore Print:** White. **Fruiting:** Solitary, scattered, or in groups under conifers, especially spruce and pine; summer, fall, early winter. **Range:** Northeastern N. America and Pacific Coast. **Family:** Hygrophoraceae. **Comments:** Although listed as edible, it has poor flavor. **Similar Species:** Tawny Almond Waxy Cap (*H. bakerensis*; edible) has a yellowish brown cap and an almond odor. Dusky Waxy Cap (*H. camarophyllus*; edible) has a dark brownish gray cap, a pale brownish gray stalk, and an odor of coal tar.

◀ *Clitocybe sclerotoidea*

▼ *Lentinus adhaerens*

▼ Gray Almond Waxy Cap
  Hygrophorus agathosmus

OTHER MUSHROOMS

Poison Pie, *Hebeloma crustuliniforme* POISONOUS

Cap: 3–8 cm wide; convex; with an inrolled edge in young specimens; smooth, sticky; creamy white, with dull yellow-brown over the center. Flesh thick, firm, white; odor radish-like; taste bitter. **Gills:** Attached to the stalk and notched; closely spaced; appearing fine-toothed; white to pale gray, developing brown dots along the edges when dry. **Stalk:** 3–8 cm long, 5–10 mm thick, equal in thickness overall to somewhat bulbous near the base; white; upper portion covered with minute, soft, white scales; interior solid. **Spore Print:** Brown. **Fruiting:** Scattered or in groups on the ground in urban areas or mixed woods; fall, winter, spring. **Range:** Widely distributed in N. America. **Family:** Cortinariaceae. **Comments:** This is a large genus with many poisonous members; *Hebeloma* species, therefore, should not be collected for the table. **Similar Species:** *H. sinapizans* (poisonous) also has a radish-like odor and taste but is darker brown and larger. *Inocybe olpidiocystis* (edibility unknown) has a yellowish-brown cap and a solid, white stalk that is equal in thickness overall; it lacks the minute, soft, white scales on the stalk and the radish-like odor.

Lead Poisoner, *Entoloma sinuatum* POISONOUS

Cap: 7–15 cm wide; convex to nearly flat with age, sometimes with a knob at the center; edge inrolled when young; smooth, slippery when wet; dull grayish brown. Flesh moderately thick, firm, dull white, changing to dark brown with maturity; odor and taste farinaceous (metallic-mealy). **Gills:** Attached to the stalk, notched near the stalk, closely spaced; pale gray to grayish yellow in young specimens, aging to dull pink. **Stalk:** 3–12 cm long, 1–2.5 cm thick, nearly equal in thickness overall; smooth to slightly roughened; white to pale gray. **Spore Print:** Salmon pink. **Fruiting:** Scattered or in groups on the ground in conifer and hardwood forests; fall. **Range:** Widely distributed in N. America. **Family:** Entolomataceae. **Comments:** Also known as *E. lividum*. Known to cause gastrointestinal distress. **Similar Species:** Aborted Entoloma (*E. abortivum;* edible, caution) has a grayish brown cap, a dull white stalk, and pink gills that descend the stalk; it is often found with dull white, irregularly rounded masses of aborted specimens (also edible).

Blewit, *Clitocybe nuda* EDIBLE, choice (caution)

Cap: 5–15 cm wide; broadly convex to nearly flat with age; with a wavy edge; smooth, dry; grayish violet, becoming pinkish-brown. Flesh moderately thick, firm, pale violet to grayish violet; odor fragrant. **Gills:** Attached to the stalk, notched; closely spaced; pale violet, aging to pinkish brown. **Stalk:** 3–7 cm long, 1–2.5 cm thick; becoming bulbous at the base; dry, somewhat scaly; pale lilac to brownish lilac. **Spore Print:** Pale pink. **Fruiting:** Solitary or in groups on lawns, compost piles, sawdust piles, and wood chips and in leaf litter; summer, fall (also winter in Calif.). **Range:** Widely distributed in N. America. **Family:** Tricholomataceae. **Comments:** Also known as *Lepista nuda*. This mushroom has been reported to cause gastric discomfort when consumed raw; it should therefore be cooked before being eaten. **Similar Species:** *C. irina* (edible, choice) has a dry, white cap and white to pale pink gills; it grows under conifers and hardwoods. *C. tarda* (edibility unknown) is smaller, thinner, and pinkish purple; it grows on wood chips and manured grass and in mixed woods.

▲ Poison Pie
Hebeloma crustuliniforme

▲ Lead Poisoner, *Entoloma sinuatum*

▲ Blewit, *Clitocybe nuda*

OTHER MUSHROOMS

Anise-scented Clitocybe, *Clitocybe odora*   EDIBLE

Cap: 3–9 cm wide; convex to nearly flat with age, sometimes slightly depressed at the center; with an inrolled cap edge in young specimens; dry, silky; greenish blue, fading to nearly white. Flesh moderately thick, firm, white; odor of anise (licorice); taste anise-like or mild. **Gills:** Attached to the stalk, partially descending the stalk in some specimens; closely spaced; white to pale pinkish brown. **Stalk:** 2–6 cm long, 4–12 mm thick, nearly equal in thickness overall; nearly smooth, dry; dull white. **Spore Print:** Pinkish cream. **Fruiting:** Scattered or in groups on the ground in hardwood and mixed forests; summer, fall (into winter in Calif.). **Range:** Widely distributed in N. America. **Family:** Tricholomataceae. **Comments:** The color varies depending upon age, moisture, and habitat. The greenish blue color quickly fades in hot, dry weather. **Similar Species:** *C. odora* var. *pacifica* (edible) is greenish blue overall, with some brownish tints near the cap center; it grows under conifers. *C. aeruginosa* (edibility unknown) has a grayish green cap with brown near the center, which fades to a dull white, and lacks the anise odor; it grows under hardwoods and forms a white spore print.

Purple-gilled Laccaria, *Laccaria ochropurpurea*   EDIBLE

Cap: 4–16 cm wide; convex to nearly flat with age, sometimes with a depression in the center; with a wavy edge in older specimens; dry, smooth; grayish white to purple-brown. Flesh thin to moderately thick, firm, grayish white. **Gills:** Attached to the stalk, widely spaced; thick-edged; pale purple to dark purple. **Stalk:** 5–15 cm long, 1–2 cm thick, nearly equal in thickness overall; often curved; dry, smooth to slightly roughened; grayish white to purple-brown, with longitudinal lines. **Spore Print:** Pale lilac. **Fruiting:** Solitary or scattered on the ground in hardwood forests, along roadsides, and in grassy areas; summer, fall. **Range:** Eastern N. America. **Family:** Tricholomataceae. **Comments:** The combination of a large grayish white to purple-brown cap with thick, widely spaced, purple gills is characteristic. **Similar Species:** Amethyst Laccaria (*L. amethystina;* edible) is smaller, with a lilac to purple color overall. Common Laccaria (*L. laccata;* edible) has a pinkish brown cap and pinkish gills. *L. bicolor* (edibility unknown) has a pinkish brown cap and pinkish lilac to flesh-colored gills; it occurs in western N. America.

Laccaria amethysteo-occidentalis   EDIBILITY UNKNOWN

Cap: 1–8 cm wide; convex to flat, often depressed in the center; edge inrolled, aging to decurved; covered with fine fibrils; deep purple, fading quickly in hot weather or when picked to lilac-drab and finally pale yellowish pink. Flesh thin, colored like the cap. **Gills:** Attached to the stalk, widely spaced; thick; somewhat waxy looking; consistently violet to lavender (color does not change with age). **Stalk:** 1.8–11.5 cm long, 3–12 mm wide; equal in thickness overall or narrowly club-shaped; longitudinally streaked with some scales; purple to violet, with occasional white splotches and violet hairs at the base; interior solid. **Spore Print:** White. **Fruiting:** Scattered or in small groups under conifers, often Douglas-fir; fall, winter. **Range:** Western N. America. **Family:** Tricholomataceae. **Similar Species:** Amethyst Laccaria (*L. amethystina;* edible) is similarly colored; it occurs in the forests of eastern N. America. *L. vinaceo-brunnea* (edibility unknown), which occurs only along the Gulf Coast under live oak, is purple-lilac when young but quickly turns lilac-brown to reddish.

▲ Anise-scented Clitocybe
  Clitocybe odora

▲ Purple-gilled Laccaria
  Laccaria ochropurpurea

*Laccaria
  amethysteo-occidentalis* ▶

OTHER MUSHROOMS

Common Laccaria, *Laccaria laccata*   EDIBLE

Cap: 2–6 cm wide; convex to nearly flat with age; typically sunken near the center; smooth to somewhat roughened; moist when fresh, quickly becoming dry; orange-brown to pinkish orange. Flesh thin, pinkish orange. **Gills:** Attached to the stalk, slightly descending the stalk in some specimens; widely spaced; pinkish orange to pinkish brown. **Stalk:** 2–10 cm long, 3–8 mm thick, nearly equal in thickness overall; sometimes with twisted longitudinal lines; fibrous, tough; pinkish brown. **Spore Print:** White. **Fruiting:** Solitary or in groups on the ground in conifer and hardwood forests and among mosses; summer, fall. **Range:** Widely distributed in N. America. **Family:** Tricholomataceae. **Comments:** Fresh specimens have excellent flavor and are delicious in soups and stews. **Similar Species:** Purple-gilled Laccaria (*L. ochropurpurea;* edible) has a grayish white to purple-brown cap and purple gills. Sandy Laccaria (*L. trullisata;* edible) has a pinkish brown cap, a sand-covered brownish stalk, and pinkish purple gills. Amethyst Laccaria (*L. amethystina;* edible) has purple gills, cap, and stalk.

Rooted Oudemansiella, *Oudemansiella radicata*   EDIBLE

Cap: 3–12 cm wide; convex to nearly flat with age, with a low, broad knob at the center; smooth to somewhat wrinkled, sticky; grayish white to dark brown. Flesh thin, white. **Gills:** Attached to the stalk, widely spaced; with thick edges; white. **Stalk:** 5–25 cm long, 5–10 mm thick, enlarging somewhat toward the base; dry; streaked white to grayish brown; with a long, tapering, underground, root-like base. **Spore Print:** White. **Fruiting:** Solitary or in groups on the ground in hardwood forests and on lawns; summer, fall. **Range:** Eastern N. America, west to Texas. **Family:** Tricholomataceae. **Comments:** Also known as *Collybia radicata*. The long, root-like base is easily broken and left behind when this mushroom is collected. **Similar Species:** Platterful Mushroom (*Tricholomopsis platyphylla;* edible for most individuals, caution) has a grayish brown cap, a white stalk, and white cords at the stalk base; it grows on or near wood. *Oudemansiella longipes* (edible) has a small, velvety, dry, brown cap.

Spotted Collybia, *Collybia maculata*   EDIBLE

Cap: 5–15 cm wide; convex to nearly flat with age; dry, smooth; white to pale yellow, developing reddish streaks and spots. Flesh thick, firm, white; taste bitter. **Gills:** Attached to the stalk when young, nearly free of the stalk in older specimens; closely spaced; off-white with reddish spots. **Stalk:** 5–12 cm long, 5–15 mm thick, equal in thickness overall; dry; white to pale yellow; interior hollow. **Spore Print:** Pale pink. **Fruiting:** Solitary or in groups on the ground or on rotting conifer wood; summer, fall. **Range:** Eastern N. America. **Family:** Tricholomataceae. **Comments:** Although listed as edible, this mushroom has poor flavor and is not widely collected for the table. **Similar Species:** All *Tricholoma* species form a white spore print.

Common Laccaria ▶
Laccaria laccata

▼ Rooted Oudemansiella
Oudemansiella radicata

Spotted Collybia ▶
Collybia maculata

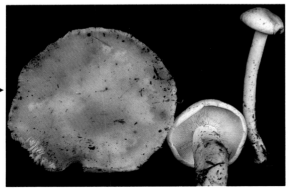

OTHER MUSHROOMS

Oak-loving Collybia, *Collybia dryophila* EDIBLE

Cap: 2–5 cm wide; convex to nearly flat; edge often upturned in older specimens; smooth; yellowish brown to reddish brown. Flesh thin, watery, white. **Gills:** Attached to the stalk, notched near the stalk, closely spaced; white to cream white. **Stalk:** 2–8 cm long, 2–5 mm thick, equal in thickness overall; smooth; yellowish brown to reddish brown; with numerous white threads attached to the base. **Spore Print:** White. **Fruiting:** Solitary or in groups on the ground in conifer and hardwood forests; spring, summer, fall. **Range:** Widely distributed in N. America. **Family:** Tricholomataceae. **Comments:** This mushroom is occasionally parasitized by a yellowish, brain-like fungus called the Collybia Jelly (*Syzygospora mycetophila* = *Christiansenia mycetophila*; edibility unknown). **Similar Species:** *Collybia subsulphurea* (edible) has a dark reddish brown cap and sulphur yellow gills and stalk; it forms a white spore print. *C. butyracea* (edible) has a slippery, reddish brown cap and forms a pale pink spore print. Hairy-stalked Collybia (*C. spongiosa*; edibility unknown) has a reddish brown cap and a stalk with reddish brown hairs; it forms a white spore print.

Lyophyllum montanum EDIBILITY UNKNOWN

Cap: 2–6.5 cm wide; convex; with cap edge incurved when young, becoming flat to uplifted with age; often with a broad central knob; gray, with a very thin, whitish bloom (like a thin wash), becoming pale brown with age. Flesh relatively thick, solid, pallid. **Gills:** Attached to (nearly free of) the stalk; closely spaced; gray. **Stalk:** 3–7 cm long, 1–1.6 cm thick, equal in thickness overall; gray, with a thin, whitish bloom (like the cap's); with a white, cottony mat at the base. **Spore Print:** White. **Fruiting:** Solitary, scattered, or in small groups in humus under spruce and fir and in association with melting snow; late spring, early summer. **Range:** At higher elevations throughout western N. America. **Family:** Tricholomataceae. **Comments:** A characteristic element of the snowbank mushroom flora. **Similar Species:** *Melanoleuca graminicola* (edibility unknown) grows in the same habitat; it has a dark to pale brown cap, pallid gills, and a brown-tinged stalk.

Yellowish White Melanoleuca, *Melanoleuca alboflavida* EDIBLE

Cap: 5–10 cm wide; bell-shaped, becoming nearly flat with age, often with a knob in the center; smooth, dry; yellow-brown, fading to dull yellow or nearly cream white. Flesh moderately thick, firm, white. **Gills:** Attached to the stalk, crowded together; white. **Stalk:** 3–15 cm long, 5–15 mm thick; straight, slender, sometimes enlarged near the base; dull white or pale brown. **Spore Print:** White. **Fruiting:** Scattered or in groups on the ground among leaves and debris in hardwood forests; summer, fall. **Range:** Eastern N. America. **Family:** Tricholomataceae. **Comments:** The general appearance of a long, slender stalk and a wide cap is characteristic of the genus. **Similar Species:** Changeable Melanoleuca (*M. melaleuca*; edible) has a slender, straight, white stalk with darker fibers; it usually grows on lawns and in disturbed areas. Straight-stalked Entoloma (*Entoloma strictius*; poisonous) has a grayish brown cap with a knob, pinkish gills, and a straight stalk with twisted brownish streaks.

▲ Oak-loving Collybia, *Collybia dryophila*

▲ *Lyophyllum montanum*

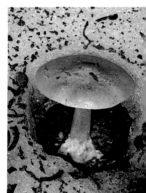

▲ *Lyophyllum montanum*

▼ Yellowish White Melanoleuca, *Melanoleuca alboflavida*

OTHER MUSHROOMS

Velvet Foot, *Flammulina velutipes*   EDIBLE

Cap: 2–5 cm wide; convex to nearly flat with age; with an inrolled edge in young specimens; smooth; sticky; reddish yellow to reddish brown. Flesh thick, firm, white to pale yellow. **Gills:** Attached to the stalk, closely spaced; white to pale yellow. **Stalk:** 2–6 cm long, 3–5 mm thick, narrowing near the base; pale yellow near the apex, densely covered with short, brown to brownish black hairs below. **Spore Print:** White. **Fruiting:** Solitary to clustered on hardwood stumps and logs; year-round. **Range:** Widely distributed in N. America. **Family:** Tricholomataceae. **Comments:** This mushroom often fruits during the winter months during thaws. The stalk can be tough and should be discarded. **Similar Species:** All *Pholiota* species form rusty brown spore prints. Deadly Galerina (*Galerina autumnalis;* deadly) has a fibrous ring on the stalk and forms a brown spore print. Fuzzy Foot (*Xeromphalina campanella;* edibility unknown) has a fuzzy brown stalk base and occurs on conifer logs and stumps; Kauffman's Xeromphalina (*X. kauffmanii;* edibility unknown) occurs on hardwood logs and stumps. Both are much smaller than *Flammulina velutipes* and have an orange-brown depressed cap and gills that descend the stalk.

Marasmius nigrodiscus   EDIBILITY UNKNOWN

Cap: 3–11 cm wide; convex to nearly flat with age; grayish yellow to yellow-brown, fading to ivory; with a broad, brownish knob at the center; with short lines visible at the cap edge. Flesh thin, soft, whitish. **Gills:** Attached to the stalk, notched near the stalk, somewhat separated; white to dull yellow. **Stalk:** 5–10 cm long, 3–12 mm thick, nearly equal in thickness overall; often with fine grooves; dry; white. **Spore Print:** White. **Fruiting:** Solitary, scattered, or in clusters on the ground under hardwoods or in mixed forests; summer, early fall. **Range:** Collected in eastern N. America; exact range limits are unknown. **Family:** Tricholomataceae. **Similar Species:** Fused Marasmius (*M. cohaerens;* edibility unknown) has a yellowish brown cap and a yellow to brownish stalk that is often fused at the base with other stalks; it grows on rotting hardwoods. Orange-Yellow Marasmius (*M. strictipes;* edibility unknown) has a yellowish orange cap, pale yellow gills, and a dull white stalk; it grows on fallen leaves.

Fairy Ring Mushroom, *Marasmius oreades*   EDIBLE (caution)

Cap: 1–5 cm wide; bell-shaped to convex; with an upturned, wavy edge in older specimens; smooth, slippery; yellowish brown to dull white. Flesh thick, white; odor mild to fruity. **Gills:** Attached to the stalk, becoming free in older specimens; somewhat separated; white to pale yellow. **Stalk:** 2–8 cm long, 2–6 mm thick, equal in thickness overall; sometimes twisted; smooth or slightly hairy; yellowish brown or reddish brown. **Spore Print:** White. **Fruiting:** Solitary or in groups or fairy rings on lawns and in fields; early summer to fall (also winter in Calif.). **Range:** Widely distributed in N. America. **Family:** Tricholomataceae. **Comments:** Be certain to avoid similar poisonous species also growing on grass. **Similar Species:** Sweating Mushroom (*Clitocybe dealbata;* poisonous) has a white, convex to depressed cap, white gills, and a white stalk; it grows on grass and in woods. Crowded White Clitocybe (*C. dilatata;* poisonous) is also white; it grows in clusters along roads and on grass. Caesar's Fiber Head (*Inocybe caesariata;* poisonous) has a hairy, yellowish brown cap and forms a brown spore print; it grows on grass.

▲ Velvet Foot, *Flammulina velutipes*

Marasmius nigrodiscus ▶

▼ Fairy Ring Mushroom, *Marasmius oreades*

OTHER MUSHROOMS

Yellow Pluteus, *Pluteus admirabilis*   EDIBLE

Cap: 1–3 cm wide; convex to nearly flat with age, with a low knob at the center; bright yellow-orange to yellowish brown, with short lines visible at the cap edge when moist. Flesh thin, fragile, dull white. **Gills:** Free of the stalk, closely spaced; white when young, aging to pink. **Stalk:** 3–6 cm long, 1–3 mm thick, nearly equal in thickness overall; fragile, watery; bright yellow, white near the base. **Spore Print:** Salmon pink. **Fruiting:** Solitary or in groups on decaying logs and stumps of hardwoods; summer, fall. **Range:** Eastern N. America. **Family:** Pluteaceae. **Comments:** The stalk of this mushroom often splits. Although edible, this species is not usually found in sufficient abundance to gather for the table. **Similar Species:** *P. flavofuligineus* (edibility unknown) has a yellowish brown cap with a brown center, lacks distinct lines, and has a dull yellow stalk; it grows on hardwood debris. Golden Granular Pluteus (*P. aurantiorugosus;* edible) has a granular, bright reddish orange cap with a small knob; it has pink gills and a white to yellow stalk that shades to reddish near the base.

Pluteus petasatus   EDIBLE

Cap: 4–10 cm wide; broadly convex to nearly flat with age; usually with a broad knob in the center; dull white, with brown scales or short hairs, especially over the center. Flesh thin, soft, white; odor and taste slightly radish-like. **Gills:** Free of the stalk, closely spaced; white in young specimens, becoming pink in older ones. **Stalk:** 4–10 cm long, 5–15 mm thick, enlarging somewhat near the base; smooth, dry; white to dull yellow-brown, especially near the base. **Spore Print:** Pink. **Fruiting:** Solitary or in clusters on wood chips, sawdust piles, and rotting wood; summer, fall. **Range:** Widely distributed in N. America. **Family:** Pluteaceae. **Comments:** This is one of several mushrooms that belong to the *P. cervinus* complex. Some are difficult to separate, but all are edible. **Similar Species:** *P. pellitus* (edible) has a dull white cap, lacks brown scales or hairs, and grows on decaying hardwood. Fawn Mushroom (*P. cervinus* = *P. atricapillus;* edible) has a tan to brown cap and a white stalk; it grows on rotting wood. *P. magnus* (edible) is larger and has a wrinkled, dark brown cap; it grows on wood. Black-edged Pluteus (*P. atromarginatus;* edible) has a dark brown cap and brownish black gill edges.

Yellow Bolbitius, *Bolbitius vitellinus*   EDIBLE

Cap: 2–5 cm wide; conical to bell-shaped with age; smooth, sticky to somewhat slimy; with narrow grooves, especially on older specimens; yellow to yellow-brown. Flesh thin, soft, yellowish. **Gills:** Attached to or free of the stalk; pale yellow in young specimens, becoming brown with age. **Stalk:** 4–8 cm long, 2–4 mm thick, nearly equal in thickness overall; smooth, with fine hairs near the apex; creamy white to pale yellow. **Spore Print:** Rusty brown. **Fruiting:** Solitary or in large clusters on dung, in grass, and on compost; spring, summer, fall. **Range:** Widely distributed in N. America. **Family:** Bolbitiaceae. **Comments:** This mushroom closely resembles *Coprinus* species; it does not form a black spore print, however, and the gills do not liquefy. **Similar Species:** *Bolbitius coprophilus* (edibility unknown) is nearly identical, but it has a pinkish brown to tan cap and a white stem with pinkish coloration near the apex.

▲ Yellow Pluteus, *Pluteus admirabilis*

▲ *Pluteus petasatus*

▲ Yellow Bolbitius, *Bolbitius vitellinus*

OTHER MUSHROOMS

Mica Cap, *Coprinus micaceus* EDIBLE

Cap: 1–5 cm wide; oval to bell-shaped, aging to convex; yellow-brown to red-brown; covered at the center with yellowish granules (often washed off by rain); smooth, with shallow grooves near the cap edge. Flesh thin, soft, white. **Gills:** Attached to the stalk, very crowded; white when young, aging to gray, then black, and dissolving away with age. **Stalk:** 2–8 cm long, 2–5 mm thick; interior hollow; white; without a ring. **Spore Print:** Black. **Fruiting:** In large clusters on hardwood stumps, along roadsides, and in grass on buried wood; spring, summer, fall. **Range:** Throughout N. America. **Family:** Coprinaceae. **Comments:** Also commonly called an inky cap. Unless cooked, true inky caps (genus *Coprinus*) dissolve away, even when refrigerated. **Similar Species:** *C. bisporus* (edible) is nearly identical but lacks the yellowish cap granules and has only two spores per basidium. Scaly Inky Cap (*C. variegatus* = *C. quadrifidus*; edibility not clearly established) has a grayish brown cap with dull white to brownish scales; its odor is disagreeable. Trooping Crumble Cap (*C. disseminatus*; edible) has smaller, brownish gray caps and white gills that turn black but do not dissolve away; it always grows in large clusters on rotting wood (sometimes buried wood).

Scarlet Waxy Cap, *Hygrophorus coccineus* EDIBLE

Cap: 2–8 cm wide; conical, aging to convex, sometimes with a small knob in the center; with an inrolled edge in younger specimens; smooth; bright red. Flesh thin, yellowish orange. **Gills:** Attached to the stalk, somewhat separated; waxy; yellowish orange to reddish orange. **Stalk:** 2–8 cm long, 2–8 mm thick; equal in thickness overall; sometimes flattened; red to yellowish orange, pale yellow near the base. **Spore Print:** White. **Fruiting:** Solitary, scattered, or clustered on the ground in conifer and hardwood forests; summer, fall. **Range:** Eastern N. America and West Coast. **Family:** Hygrophoraceae. **Comments:** This mushroom often grows in association with mosses. **Similar Species:** Fading Scarlet Waxy Cap (*H. miniatus*; edible) has a smaller, bright red cap that fades to yellowish orange. *H. puniceus* (edible) has a sticky cap and attached gills that are notched near the stalk. *H. turundus* (edibility unknown) is smaller, has a roughened cap, and is found among sphagnum moss in bogs.

California Parrot Mushroom, *Hygrophorus psittacinus*
var. *californicus* EDIBLE

Cap: 1–4 cm wide; nearly conical, aging to convex to nearly flat, with a broad, low knob; edge with fine, translucent lines; slimy; bluish with a reddish brown center when young, becoming paler with pink, pinkish gray, and olive areas. Flesh thin. **Gills:** Varying from attached to the stalk to nearly free, somewhat separated; waxy; pale tan-pink with a bluish cast, gradually aging to pale yellow. **Stalk:** 3–7 cm long, 2–6 mm thick; equal in thickness overall; slimy; bluish above, yellow to pale orange below; interior hollow. **Spore Print:** Pale yellow. **Fruiting:** Solitary, scattered, or in small groups under conifers; fall. **Range:** Calif. (and perhaps Mich.). **Family:** Hygrophoraceae. **Similar Species:** The more typical variety, Parrot Mushroom (*H. psittacinus* var. *psittacinus*; edible), occurs throughout N. America; it is slimy and has dark olive or other green shades throughout but becomes yellow as it ages or dries out. If the green color fades, it can be confused with the widely distributed *H. laetus* (edibility unknown), which has a slimy, orange to olive-orange cap and stalk, pinkish-tinged gills, and a fishy to skunk-like odor.

▲ Mica Cap, *Coprinus micaceus*

▲ Scarlet Waxy Cap, *Hygrophorus coccineus*

▼ California Parrot Mushroom
  Hygrophorus psittacinus var. *californicus*

OTHER MUSHROOMS

Rosy-Brown Waxy Cap, *Hygrophorus roseibrunneus* EDIBLE

Cap: 2–10 cm wide; convex, becoming flat to uplifted with age; with a broad, low central knob; smooth, sticky when wet; dark pinkish brown to pinkish cinnamon, paler toward the cap edge and paler overall in older specimens. Flesh thick at the center, thin elsewhere, soft, white. **Gills:** Attached to the stalk, closely spaced; waxy; white. **Stalk:** 3–12 cm long, 4–18 mm thick, equal in thickness overall; covered above with dust-like particles and minute fibrils, sticky near the base when wet; white; with a slight partial veil that leaves no pronounced ring. **Spore Print:** White. **Fruiting:** Scattered or in groups under conifers and hardwoods; fall, winter. **Range:** Throughout N. America. **Family:** Hygrophoraceae. **Comments:** This is an especially common species under oak. **Similar Species:** Bitter Leucopax (*Leucopaxillus amarus*; inedible) has similar coloration, but it is larger, has a dry cap, and exhibits a bitter taste.

Witch's Hat, *Hygrophorus conicus* var. *atrosanguineus* POISONOUS

Cap: 2–9 cm wide; conical to bell-shaped, often with a small knob in the center; smooth, sticky; dark strawberry red to violet-brown, bruising black. Flesh thin, reddish orange, bruising black; odor strongly aromatic. **Gills:** Free of the stalk, closely spaced; pale yellow to greenish orange, bruising black. **Stalk:** 4–16 cm long, 5–15 mm thick; smooth; yellow to yellowish orange, pale yellow near the base, bruising black. **Spore Print:** White. **Fruiting:** Solitary, scattered, or in groups on the ground under conifers and hardwoods; summer, fall (also winter in Calif.). **Range:** Widely distributed in N. America. **Family:** Hygrophoraceae. **Comments:** The stalk may be twisted in some specimens. The combination of a conical cap together with the tendency of all parts to bruise black is characteristic of the species. **Similar Species:** *H. conicus* var. *conicus* (poisonous) is nearly identical (and also bruises black), but it has a silky, bright red cap and lacks the aromatic odor. *H. acutoconicus* (edibility unknown) has a bright yellow to yellowish orange cap and does not bruise black. *H. cuspidatus* (edibility unknown) has a scarlet cap and a yellowish orange stalk. *H. spadiceus* (edibility unknown) has a yellowish brown cap, yellow gills, and a yellow stalk; it grows on the ground in burned areas. The last 2 species also fail to bruise black.

Kauffman's Phaeocollybia, *Phaeocollybia kauffmanii*
EDIBILITY UNKNOWN

Cap: 8–19.5 cm wide; broadly conical to convex, aging to nearly flat, with a central knob; cap edge inrolled; smooth, slimy; cinnamon, reddish cinnamon, or reddish brown, fading with age to reddish orange. Flesh thick, firm, dark brown; taste and odor somewhat farinaceous (metallic-mealy). **Gills:** Free of the stalk or nearly so, closely spaced; dirty cream, aging to dark reddish brown. **Stalk:** 10–40 cm long, 1.5–4 cm thick, tapering below; anchored in thick conifer humus by a long, root-like base; smooth; pallid above, dull purplish brown below. **Spore Print:** Pale cinnamon brown. **Fruiting:** Scattered or in groups in thick humus under conifers; very late summer, fall. **Range:** Pacific Coast; also known from Tenn. **Family:** Cortinariaceae. **Comments:** This and other species of *Phaeocollybia* (all of unknown edibility) are primarily associated with western conifers. **Similar Species:** Rooting Redwood Collybia (*Collybia umbonata*, also known as *Caulorhiza umbonata*; edibility unknown) occurs in Calif. under redwood. *Oudemansiella radicata* (edible) occurs in eastern N. America (west to Texas) under hardwoods. Both are "rooting" species but are less robust and form white spore prints.

▲ Rosy-Brown Waxy Cap, *Hygrophorus roseibrunneus*

▲ Witch's Hat
Hygrophorus conicus
var. *atrosanguineus*

Kauffman's
   Phaeocollybia ▶
*Phaeocollybia
kauffmanii*

Chemical Testing
of Spores in Identification

Unless you have a microscope at your disposal, work with spores is usually limited to determining spore color from a spore print. However, there is another important spore characteristic that you can quickly and easily discover without the aid of a microscope—the reaction of spores with Melzer's reagent.

Similar to the way iodine can be used to detect the presence of starch, Melzer's reagent, a special iodine-containing solution, is employed to test for chemical differences in the composition of mushroom spore walls. Although the chemicals in the cell walls that react with the reagent are not fully understood, the color changes that result from the reaction are consistent, thus making the test useful in identification of gilled mushrooms. The changes are described in the following terms:

amyloid: a change to blue-black, violet-black, or black; usually occurs very rapidly (pale gray to blue to violet-black under the microscope)

dextrinoid (also called *pseudoamyloid*): a change to pale to dark reddish brown (yellowish brown to orange-brown to pale or dark rusty brown to reddish brown under the microscope)

inamyloid (also called *nonamyloid*): little or no color change (colorless to pale yellow under the microscope)

This test is especially useful as an auxiliary identification aid for mushrooms with white or light-colored spores, and in some cases it can be used to help differentiate between otherwise similar genera or species. For example, species of *Amanita*, all of which have either amyloid or inamyloid spores, can be distinguished from the large species of *Lepiota*, which have dextrinoid spores. Likewise, the False Chanterelle (*Hygrophoropsis aurantiaca*), a look-alike of some true chanterelles, has dextrinoid spores, whereas the chanterelles are inamyloid. The Melzer's reagent color reactions of the spores of all mushrooms illustrated, described, or noted under "Similar Species" in this guide are listed (along with other spore data) in tables at the back of the book.

To make the Melzer's reagent test on spores, follow the instructions below.

1. Obtain a good spore print, as described in the introduction to this book. It is best to make a part of the spore print on a glass slide or glass (or plastic) coverslip.

2. Using another clean slide or coverslip as a tool, scrape the spores into a small pile. **NOTE:** Spores can be scraped from paper, but paper fibers themselves usually produce a rapid amyloid reaction that will interfere with the testing of spores.

3. Hold the slide or coverslip over a piece of white paper (reflected light

from the paper will help illuminate the spores). Place a drop of Melzer's reagent near (but not touching) the spores.

4. Tilt the glass to slowly run the solution into the spores, and *simultaneously*, through a hand lens or a magnifying glass, observe any color change that takes place. Most changes, if any, will be rapid.

5. If no change occurs, check again after a few minutes (do not let the spores dry out).

6. Compare your results with information provided in the descriptions and the spore data tables in this book. Be sure to record the results for future reference.

Melzer's reagent can be made from the following:

Iodine crystals	0.5 grams
Potassium iodide	1.5 grams
Chloral hydrate	20.0 grams
Distilled water	20.0 milliliters

Mix the chemicals together, gently warm (*but do not boil*) them until all solids are dissolved, and then cool. The solution can be stored in a tightly capped bottle and is most easily dispensed from some form of dropper.

In the United States and Canada, chloral hydrate is a legally controlled substance and can be obtained only with a proper government permit. Local mushroom clubs and professional mycologists may be a source of ready-made solution. It is also sold in ready-made form by some commercial sources.

Microscopic Spore Characteristics

Many species of fungi are easy to identify from their field (macroscopic) characters alone, but many more require examination of anatomical (microscopic) features. Macroscopic features are often subjective and sometimes difficult to interpret. In some cases, they may be influenced by environmental conditions (including nutrient availability, temperature, rainfall, humidity, day length) or by specimen age or both. Color, for example, sometimes varies with the conditions under which the specimen grows, with its age, and with the color perception of the observer. Preliminary identifications made by means of macroscopic characters can often be easily confirmed if one has access to a microscope. Further, many species of mushrooms that have nearly identical macroscopic features, and thus resist identification in the field, are easily differentiated by microscopic examination. A number of different microscopic characters, among them the microscopic features of spores, are used by mycologists to help in the precise identification of mushrooms. Thus, a good quality microscope with an oil-immersion lens is a valuable investment for the serious enthusiast. It will provide a wealth of important additional information for the identification of mushrooms.

Although this guide emphasizes macroscopic features, information about the microscopic features of spores of all species described (including those noted as similar species) is presented here in table form for those with access to a microscope.

Spore shape refers to the overall form of the spore. Spore size (measured in the microscope by means of a ruler-like device called an ocular micrometer) is expressed as the ranges of length and width (length range × width range) in micrometers. Microscopic color refers to the general color of the spore when mounted in water or dilute (3%) KOH solution and viewed with the microscope. In general, because of the illumination and optics involved, color through the microscope tends to be paler than that obtained from a spore print; likewise, colors also vary somewhat, but they should be near that noted. Hyaline means colorless, lacking pigment; such a spore will appear colorless or with a slight pale green tinge (caused by refraction). The Melzer's reaction is a notation of the color change, if any, of the spores when mounted in Melzer's reagent: amyloid = spores becoming blue-black; dextrinoid = spores becoming reddish brown to orange-brown; inamyloid = no change in color (spores will appear pale yellow due to the uptake of the Melzer's solution). Surface features refer to visible characteristics of the spore wall (some have an apical germ pore) and its surface (smooth, or decorated with various appendages—wrinkles, warts, spines, isolated ridges, ridges forming a network, and other features).

SPORE DATA

GENUS AND SPECIES	SPORE SHAPE	SPORE SIZE (in micrometers)	MICROSCOPIC COLOR	MELZER'S REACTION	SURFACE FEATURES
Agaricus arvensis	elliptical	7–9 × 4.5–6	brown	inamyloid	smooth
augustus	short-elliptical	8–11 × 5–6.5	brown	inamyloid	smooth
bitorquis	oval to globose	5–6 × 4–5	brown	inamyloid	smooth
campestris	elliptical	5.5–7.5 × 3.5–5	brown	inamyloid	smooth, with apical pore
fusco-fibrillosus	elliptical	4.9–7.5 × 3.4–5.3	brown	inamyloid	smooth
haemorrhoidarius	elliptical	5.3–6 × 3.9–4.4	brown	inamyloid	smooth
meleagris	oval	5–7 × 3–4	brown	inamyloid	smooth
placomyces	oval to elliptical	4.5–6 × 3.5–4.5	brown	inamyloid	smooth
pocillator	elliptical	4.5–6 × 3–3.8	pale brown	inamyloid	smooth
subrufescens	elliptical	6–7.5 × 4–5	brown	inamyloid	smooth
subrutilescens	elliptical	5–6 × 3–3.5	brown	inamyloid	smooth
xanthodermus	elliptical	5–7 × 3–4	brown	inamyloid	smooth
Agrocybe acericola	elliptical	8.5–10.5 × 5–6.5	pale yellow-brown	inamyloid	smooth, with apical pore
dura	elliptical	10–14 × 6.5–8	pale brown	inamyloid	smooth, with apical pore
praecox	elliptical	8–11 × 5–6	pale brown	inamyloid	smooth, with apical pore
Aleuria aurantia	elliptical	17–24 × 9–11	hyaline	inamyloid	covered by a coarse network
Aleurodiscus oakesii	oval to elliptical	18–21 × 12–13	hyaline	amyloid	with fine warts
Amanita bisporigera	globose	7–10	hyaline	amyloid	smooth
brunnescens	globose	8–9.5	hyaline	amyloid	smooth
caesarea	oval	8–12 × 6–8	hyaline	inamyloid	smooth
calyptrata	elliptical	9–11 × 5–6	hyaline	inamyloid	smooth
ceciliae	globose	11.5–14	hyaline	inamyloid	smooth
citrina	globose	6–7	hyaline	amyloid	smooth
flavoconia	elliptical	7–9.5 × 4.5–6	hyaline	amyloid	smooth
flavorubescens	elliptical	9.5–10.5 × 6–7	hyaline	amyloid	smooth
frostiana	globose	7–10	hyaline	amyloid	smooth
fulva	globose	9.5–12.5	hyaline	inamyloid	smooth
gemmata	elliptical	8.5–11 × 5.5–8.5	hyaline	inamyloid	smooth
hemibapha	elliptical	8–9.5 × 5.5–7	hyaline	inamyloid	smooth
muscaria	elliptical	8–11 × 6–8	hyaline	inamyloid	smooth
pantherina	elliptical	8–14 × 6.3–10	hyaline	inamyloid	smooth

142

Species	Shape	Size	Color	Amyloid reaction	Surface
parcivolvata	elliptical	9–14 × 6–8	hyaline	inamyloid	smooth
phalloides	subglobose	8.5–10 × 6.8–8	hyaline	amyloid	smooth
porphyria	globose	7–9	hyaline	amyloid	smooth
rubescens	elliptical	7–9 × 5–7	hyaline	amyloid	smooth
vaginata	globose	8–10.5	hyaline	inamyloid	smooth to finely roughened
verna	elliptical	9–12 × 6.5–8	hyaline	amyloid	smooth
virosa	globose to elliptical	8–12 × 6.5–9.5	hyaline	amyloid	smooth
Anthracobia melaloma	elliptical	14–22 × 7–11	hyaline	inamyloid	smooth
Armillaria caligata	elliptical	6–7.5 × 4.5–5.5	hyaline	inamyloid	smooth
olida	elliptical	10.5–12.5 × 5–6.7	hyaline	inamyloid	smooth
zelleri	elliptical	4–5 × 3–4	hyaline	inamyloid	smooth
Armillariella mellea	elliptical	6–9.5 × 4.5–6	hyaline	inamyloid	smooth
tabescens	elliptical	6–10 × 5–7	hyaline	inamyloid	smooth
Auricularia auricula	sausage-shaped	12–15 × 4–6	hyaline	inamyloid	minutely roughened
Auriscalpium vulgare	subglobose	5–6 × 4–5.2	hyaline	inamyloid	with apical pore, wrinkled and warted
Austroboletus betula	elliptical	15–19.5 × 7.5–10	pale yellow-brown	inamyloid	smooth
Baeospora myriadophylla	elliptical	6–7 × 3–3.5	hyaline	amyloid	smooth
Bisporella citrina	elliptical	9–14 × 3–5	hyaline	inamyloid	smooth, often 2-celled
Bjerkandera adusta	elliptical	4–5.5, × 2.5–3	hyaline	inamyloid	smooth
Bolbitius coprophilus	elliptical	12–15 × 6–8	pale yellow-brown	inamyloid	smooth, with apical pore
vitellinus	elliptical	10–13 × 6–7.5	pale yellow-brown	inamyloid	smooth, with apical pore
Boletellus chrysenteroides	elliptical	12–16 × 4.5–7.5	pale yellow	inamyloid	longitudinally striate
russelli	elliptical	15–20 × 7–11	pale yellow-brown	inamyloid	with longitudinal ridges
Boletinellus meruliodes	elliptical	7–11 × 5–7.5	pale yellow-brown	inamyloid	smooth
Boletus chrysenteron	elliptical	9–13 × 4–5	pale yellow	inamyloid	smooth
edulis	cylindrical to spindle-shaped	12–20 × 4–6.5	pale yellow-brown	inamyloid	smooth
erythropus	elliptical	12–15 × 5.6–6.5	hyaline	inamyloid	smooth
flammans	elliptical	10.5–12 × 3.5–5.5	pale yellow	inamyloid	smooth
frostii	elliptical	12–17 × 4–6	pale yellow-brown	inamyloid	smooth
modestus	elliptical	7–14 × 3.5–5	pale yellow	inamyloid	smooth
parasiticus	elliptical	12–18.5 × 3.5–5	pale brown	inamyloid	smooth
pulcherrimus	elliptical to spindle-shaped	11–16 × 5–6.5	pale yellow	inamyloid	smooth
rubroflammeus	elliptical	10–14 × 4–5	pale yellow	inamyloid	smooth
satanas	elliptical to spindle-shaped	12–15 × 4–6	hyaline	inamyloid	smooth
separans	elliptical	12.5–16 × 3.5–4.5	pale yellow	inamyloid	smooth
zelleri	elliptical	10–11 × 4–6	pale yellow	inamyloid	smooth

GENUS AND SPECIES	SPORE SHAPE	SPORE SIZE (in micrometers)	MICROSCOPIC COLOR	MELZER'S REACTION	SURFACE FEATURES
Calbovista subsculpta	globose	3–5	pale brown	inamyloid	minutely warted
Caloscypha fulgens	elliptical	10–12 × 6–8	hyaline	inamyloid	smooth
Calvatia craniformis	oval to globose	2.5–4.5 × 2.5–4.5	pale yellow	inamyloid	smooth
cyathiformis	globose	4–7	pale lilac	inamyloid	with minute spines
gigantea	oval to globose	3.5–5.5 × 3–5	pale yellow	inamyloid	smooth to minutely spiny
sculpta	globose	3.3–6.6	pale yellowish brown	inamyloid	with minute spines
subcretacea	globose	4–6.5	pale brown	inamyloid	smooth to minutely spiny
Cantharellus cibarius	elliptical	8–11 × 4–5.5	hyaline	inamyloid	smooth
cinnabarinus	elliptical	6–11 × 4–6	hyaline	inamyloid	smooth
ignicolor	elliptical	9–13 × 6–9	hyaline	inamyloid	smooth
lateritus	oval-elliptical	7–9.5 × 4.5–6	hyaline	inamyloid	smooth
subalbidus	elliptical	7–9 × 5–5.5	hyaline	inamyloid	smooth
tubaeformis	broadly elliptical	8–13 × 6–10	hyaline	inamyloid	smooth
xanthopus	elliptical	9–11 × 6–7.5	hyaline	inamyloid	smooth
Catathelasma ventricosa	elliptical	9–12 × 4–6	hyaline	inamyloid	smooth
Cerrena unicolor	elliptical	4.5–5.5 × 2.5–3.5	hyaline	inamyloid	smooth
Chlorociboria					
aeruginascens	spindle-shaped	6–10 × 1.5–2	hyaline	inamyloid	smooth
Chlorophyllum molybdites	elliptical	8–13 × 6.5–8	hyaline	dextrinoid	smooth, with apical pore
Chroogomphus leptocystis	subfusoid	12–18 × 6–7	gray	inamyloid	smooth
rutilus	subfusoid	14–22 × 6–7.5	gray	inamyloid	smooth
tomentosus	subfusoid	15–25 × 6–9	gray	inamyloid	smooth
vinicolor	subfusoid	17–25 × 4.5–7.5	gray	inamyloid	smooth
Clavaria purpurea	elliptical	5.5–9 × 3–5	hyaline	inamyloid	smooth
rubicundula	elliptical	5.5–8.5 × 3–4	hyaline	inamyloid	smooth
vermicularis	elliptical	9–13 × 5–7	hyaline	inamyloid	smooth
zollingeri	subglobose to elliptical	4–7 × 3–5	hyaline	inamyloid	smooth
Clavariadelphus ligula	elliptical	8–18 × 3–6	hyaline	inamyloid	smooth
pistillaris	elliptical	11–16 × 6–10	hyaline	inamyloid	smooth
truncatus	elliptical	4.5–6.5 × 1.5–2.5	hyaline	inamyloid	smooth
Clavicorona pyxidata	elliptical	4–5 × 2–3	hyaline	amyloid	smooth
Clavulina cinerea	oval to globose	6.5–11 × 7–10	hyaline	inamyloid	smooth
cristata	oval to globose	7–11 × 6.5–10	hyaline	inamyloid	smooth

144

Clavulinopsis fusiformis	oval to globose	5–9 × 4.5–9	hyaline	inamyloid	smooth
Clitocybe aeruginosa	elliptical	6–8 × 3.5–5	hyaline	inamyloid	smooth
dealbata	elliptical	5–6 × 3–4	hyaline	inamyloid	smooth
densifolia	oval	4–4.5 × 2.5–3.5	hyaline	inamyloid	slightly roughened
dilatata	elliptical	4.5–6.5 × 3–3.5	hyaline	inamyloid	smooth
fasciculata	elliptical	4.5–6 × 3–4	hyaline	inamyloid	slightly roughened
gibba	elliptical	5–8 × 3–5	hyaline	inamyloid	smooth
inornata	elliptical to subfusoid	8.5–10 × 2.5–3.5	hyaline	inamyloid	smooth
irina	elliptical	7–10 × 4–5	hyaline	inamyloid	smooth or slightly roughened
nuda	elliptical	5.5–8 × 3.5–5	hyaline	inamyloid	slightly roughened
odora	elliptical	6–8 × 3.5–5	hyaline	inamyloid	smooth
odora var. pacifica	elliptical	6.5–8 × 4–4.5	hyaline	inamyloid	smooth
phaeophthalma	elliptical	4.5–6.5 × 3–4	hyaline	inamyloid	smooth
sclerotoidea	subfusoid	8–11 × 3–4	hyaline	inamyloid	smooth
squamulosa	elliptical	5.5–7.5 × 3–4	hyaline	inamyloid	smooth
subconnexa	elliptical	4.5–6 × 3–3.5	hyaline	inamyloid	slightly roughened
tarda	elliptical	6–8 × 3–5	hyaline	inamyloid	smooth
Collybia butyracea	elliptical	6–9 × 3–3.5	hyaline	inamyloid	smooth
cirrhata	short-elliptical	4.5–6.5 × 2–3.5	hyaline	inamyloid	smooth
cookei	short-elliptical	4.5–5.5 × 2.5–3.5	hyaline	inamyloid	smooth
dryophila	elliptical	5–7 × 3–3.5	hyaline	inamyloid	smooth
maculata	globose to oval	5–7 × 4–5	hyaline	inamyloid	smooth
spongiosa	elliptical	6–8.5 × 3.4–4.2	hyaline	inamyloid	smooth
subsulphurea	elliptical	5.5–6.5 × 2.5–3.5	hyaline	inamyloid	smooth
tuberosa	short-elliptical	4.2–6.2 × 2.5–3.5	hyaline	inamyloid	smooth
umbonata	elliptical	5–8 × 3–5	hyaline	amyloid	smooth
Conocybe lactea	elliptical	12–14 × 6–9	pinkish brown	inamyloid	smooth, with apical pore
subovalis	elliptical	12–16 × 7–9	pale brown	inamyloid	smooth, with apical pore
tenera	elliptical	11–12 × 5.5–6.5	pale brown	inamyloid	smooth, with apical pore
Coprinus atramentarius	elliptical	8–12 × 4.5–6.5	gray-black	inamyloid	smooth, with apical pore
bisporus	elliptical	9.5–14.5 × 5.5–7.5	gray-black	inamyloid	smooth, with apical pore
brassicae	oval	6.5–7.5 × 4.5–5.5	gray-black	inamyloid	smooth, with apical pore
comatus	elliptical	13–18 × 7–8	gray-black	inamyloid	smooth, with apical pore
disseminatus	elliptical	7–10 × 4–5	gray-black	inamyloid	smooth, with apical pore
laniger	elliptical	7–10 × 4–4.5	gray-black	inamyloid	smooth, with apical pore
micaceus	elliptical	7–10 × 4–5	gray-black	inamyloid	smooth, with apical pore
radians	elliptical	8–10 × 4–6.5	gray-black	inamyloid	smooth, with apical pore

GENUS AND SPECIES	SPORE SHAPE	SPORE SIZE (in micrometers)	MICROSCOPIC COLOR	MELZER'S REACTION	SURFACE FEATURES
Coprinus sterquilinus	elliptical	17–22 × 10–13	gray-black	inamyloid	smooth, with apical pore
variegatus	elliptical	7.5–10 × 4–5	gray-black	inamyloid	smooth, with apical pore
Cordyceps capitata	cylindrical to thread-like	15–25 × 2–3	hyaline	inamyloid	smooth
melolonthae	elliptical	4–10 × 1–2.5	hyaline	inamyloid	smooth
militaris	barrel-shaped	3–6 × 1–1.5	hyaline	inamyloid	smooth
ophioglossoides	elliptical	2–5 × 1.5–2	hyaline	inamyloid	smooth
Coriolus versicolor	cylindrical	4–6 × 1.5–2	hyaline	inamyloid	smooth
Cortinarius alboviolaceus	elliptical	8–12 × 5–6.5	brown	inamyloid	minutely roughened
armillatus	elliptical	9–12 × 5.5–7.5	pale brown	inamyloid	minutely roughened
corrugatus	elliptical	10–13 × 7–9	yellow-brown	inamyloid	minutely roughened
cylindripes	almond-shaped	12–15 × 6.5–8	pale yellow	inamyloid	minutely roughened
iodeoides	elliptical	7–7.5 × 4–4.5	pale brown	inamyloid	minutely roughened
iodes	elliptical	8–12 × 5–6.5	pale brown	inamyloid	minutely roughened
salor	globose	6–9	pale yellow	inamyloid	minutely roughened
traganus	elliptical	7.5–10 × 5–6	pale brown	inamyloid	minutely roughened
violaceus	elliptical	13–17 × 8–10	yellow-brown	inamyloid	minutely roughened
Craterellus caeruleofuscus	elliptical	7–9 × 5–6.5	hyaline	inamyloid	smooth
cinereus	elliptical	7.5–11 × 4.5–6.5	hyaline	inamyloid	smooth
cornucopioides	elliptical	11–15 × 7–9	hyaline	inamyloid	smooth
fallax	elliptical	11–14 × 7–9	hyaline	inamyloid	smooth
foetidus	elliptical	8.5–13 × 5–7.5	hyaline	inamyloid	smooth
odoratus	elliptical	8.5–12 × 4.5–6.5	hyaline	inamyloid	smooth
Crepidotus applanatus	globose	4–5.5	pale yellow-brown	inamyloid	minutely spiny
versutus	elliptical	7–11 × 4.5–6	pale yellow-brown	inamyloid	minutely spiny
Crinipellis campanella	elliptical	8–9 × 4–4.5	hyaline	inamyloid	smooth
setipes	elliptical	6.7–8.9 × 3–4.5	hyaline	inamyloid	smooth
stipitaria	elliptical	6–9 × 4–8	hyaline	inamyloid	smooth
zonata	elliptical	4–6 × 3–5	hyaline	inamyloid	smooth
Crucibulum laeve	elliptical	6–10 × 4–6	hyaline	inamyloid	smooth
Cryptoporus volvatus	elliptical	8–12 × 3–5	hyaline	inamyloid	smooth
Cudonia lutea	needle-shaped	45–78 × 2–2.5	hyaline	inamyloid	smooth, many-celled
Cyathus olla	oval	10–14 × 6–8	hyaline	inamyloid	smooth
stercoreus	globose to oval	25–35 × 25–35	hyaline	inamyloid	smooth

Species	Shape	Size	Color	Reaction	Surface
striatus	elliptical	18–20 × 8–10	hyaline	inamyloid	with thick walls and apiculus
Cystoderma amianthinum fallax	elliptical	4.5–7.5 × 2.5–3.5	hyaline	amyloid	smooth
Dacrymyces palmatus	elliptical	3.5–5.5 × 2.5–3.5	hyaline	amyloid	smooth
	cylindrical to sausage-shaped	17–25 × 6–8	hyaline	inamyloid	smooth, 8- to 10-celled
Daedaleopsis confragosa	cylindrical	7–11 × 2–3	hyaline	inamyloid	smooth
Dictyophora duplicata	elliptical	3.5–4.5 × 1–2	hyaline	inamyloid	smooth
Ductifera pululahuana	oval to short-cylindrical, curved	9–12 × 4.5–7.5	hyaline	inamyloid	smooth
Endoptychum agaricoides	elliptical	6–10 × 5–7	pale yellowish brown	inamyloid	smooth
Entoloma abortivum	angular	8–10 × 5–7	hyaline	inamyloid	smooth
cetratum	angular	11–12.5 × 6.5–7.5	hyaline	inamyloid	smooth
luteum	angular	9–13 × 8–12	hyaline	inamyloid	smooth
murraii	elliptical	9–12 × 8–10	hyaline	inamyloid	smooth
salmoneum	globose to angular	10–12	hyaline	inamyloid	smooth
sinuatum	angular	7–10 × 7–9	hyaline	inamyloid	smooth
staurosporum	angular	6–8 × 1.5–2.5	hyaline	inamyloid	smooth
strictius	angular	10–13 × 7.5–9	hyaline	inamyloid	smooth
violaceum	angular	8–10 × 5.5–7.5	hyaline	inamyloid	smooth
Exidia alba	sausage-shaped	8–11 × 4–5	hyaline	inamyloid	smooth
glandulosa	sausage-shaped	10–16 × 4–5	hyaline	inamyloid	smooth
nucleata	sausage-shaped	10–11 × 4–4.5	hyaline	inamyloid	smooth
recisa	sausage-shaped	10.5–14 × 3–5	hyaline	inamyloid	smooth
Favolus alveolaris	cylindrical	9–11 × 3–3.5	hyaline	inamyloid	smooth
Fistulina hepatica	oval	4.5–6 × 3–4	hyaline	inamyloid	smooth
Flammulina velutipes	narrowly elliptical	7–9 × 3–4	hyaline	inamyloid	smooth
Fomitopsis pinicola	oval	5–7 × 4–5	hyaline	inamyloid	smooth
Fuscoboletinus ochraceoroseus	elliptical	7–9.5 × 2.5–3.5	reddish brown	inamyloid	smooth
spectabilis	elliptical	9–15 × 4.5–6.5	reddish brown	dextrinoid	smooth
Galerina autumnalis	elliptical	8.5–10.5 × 5–6.5	pale yellow-brown	inamyloid	wrinkled
venenata	oval	8–11 × 5–6.5	pale yellow-brown	inamyloid	roughened, with smooth area near base
Galiella rufa	elliptical	18–20 × 8–10	hyaline	inamyloid	finely warted, with narrow ends
Ganoderma applanatum	oval	6–9 × 4.5–6	pale brown	inamyloid	slightly roughened and truncate
curtisii	oval	9–11 × 5–7	pale brown	inamyloid	slightly roughened and truncate

GENUS AND SPECIES	SPORE SHAPE	SPORE SIZE (in micrometers)	MICROSCOPIC COLOR	MELZER'S REACTION	SURFACE FEATURES
Ganoderma lucidum	oval	7–12 × 6–8	pale brown	inamyloid	slightly roughened and truncate
oregonense	oval	10–16 × 7.5–9	pale brown	inamyloid	slightly roughened and truncate
tsugae	oval	9–11 × 6–8	pale brown	inamyloid	thick-walled and truncate
Geastrum fimbriatum	globose	3–3.5	brown	inamyloid	smooth
saccatum	globose	3.5–4.5	brown	inamyloid	minutely warted
triplex	globose	3.5–4.5	pale brown	inamyloid	minutely warted
Gloeophyllum sepiarium	cylindrical	9–13 × 3–5	hyaline	inamyloid	smooth
Gomphidius glutinosus	subfusoid	15–21 × 4–7.5	gray	inamyloid	smooth
maculatus	subfusoid	14–22 × 6–8	gray	inamyloid	smooth
oregonensis	elliptical	10–13 × 4.5–7	grayish black	inamyloid	smooth
subroseus	subfusoid	15–21 × 4.5–7	gray	inamyloid	smooth
Gomphus clavatus	elliptical	10–13 × 4–6.5	hyaline	inamyloid	warted
floccosus	elliptical	12–15 × 6–7.5	pale yellow	inamyloid	smooth to slightly wrinkled
kauffmanii	elliptical	12.5–16 × 6–7.5	pale yellow	inamyloid	with small warts
Grifola frondosa	oval	5–7 × 3.5–5	hyaline	inamyloid	smooth
Gymnopilus penetrans	elliptical	6.5–9.5 × 4–5.5	yellow-brown	inamyloid	with small warts
spectabilis	elliptical	7.5–10.5 × 4.5–6	pale yellow	inamyloid	wrinkled
Gyromitra ambigua	elliptical	22–33 × 7–12	hyaline	inamyloid	smooth, with blunt projections at each end
caroliniana	fusoid	25–30 × 12–14	hyaline	inamyloid	net-like ridges, tapered at each end
esculenta	elliptical	18–26 × 9–12	hyaline	inamyloid	smooth
fastigiata	fusoid	25–30 × 11.5–15	hyaline	inamyloid	net-like ridges, tapered at each end
gigas	oval to elliptical	26–34 × 12–15	hyaline	inamyloid	wrinkled
infula	elliptical	18–24 × 8–12	hyaline	inamyloid	smooth
Gyroporus castaneus	elliptical	8–12 × 5–6	hyaline	inamyloid	smooth
cyanescens	elliptical	8–10 × 5–6	hyaline	inamyloid	smooth
purpurinus	elliptical	8–11 × 5–6.5	hyaline	inamyloid	smooth
Hebeloma crustuliniforme	elliptical	9.5–12.5 × 5.5–7.5	pale brown	inamyloid	minutely wrinkled
sinapizans	elliptical	10–12.5 × 6–7	pale brown	inamyloid	minutely wrinkled
Helvella crispa	elliptical	18–21 × 10–13	hyaline	inamyloid	smooth
elastica	elliptical	18–22 × 11–13	hyaline	inamyloid	smooth

	Shape	Size (μm)	Color	Reaction	Surface
lacunosa	elliptical	17–20 × 11–13	hyaline	inamyloid	smooth
macropus	elliptical	20–30 × 10–12	hyaline	inamyloid	smooth
Hericium abietus	subglobose	4.5–5.5 × 4–4.5	hyaline	amyloid	smooth to minutely roughened
americanum	globose to subglobose	3–5 × 5–6	hyaline	amyloid	smooth to minutely roughened
coralloides	oval to globose	3–5 × 3–4	hyaline	amyloid	minutely roughened
erinaceus	oval to globose	5–6.5 × 4–5.5	hyaline	amyloid	smooth to minutely roughened
erinaceus	oval to globose	4.5–6 × 4–5	hyaline	amyloid	smooth to minutely roughened
ssp. *erinaceo-abietis*					
Heterobasidion annosum	globose	3–5	hyaline	inamyloid	smooth
Humaria hemisphaerica	elliptical	25–27 × 12–15	hyaline	inamyloid	with small warts
Hydnum imbricatum	globose	5–8	pale brown	inamyloid	with irregular warts
repandum	elliptical	4–5.5 × 2.5–3	hyaline	inamyloid	smooth
scabrosum	globose	5–6	pale brown	inamyloid	with irregular warts
umbilicatum	oval to globose	7.5–9 × 6–7.5	hyaline	inamyloid	smooth
Hygrophoropsis aurantiaca	elliptical	5–7 × 3–4	hyaline	dextrinoid	smooth
Hygrophorus acutoconicus	elliptical	9–15 × 5–9	hyaline	inamyloid	smooth
agathosmus	elliptical	7–10 × 4.5–5.5	hyaline	inamyloid	smooth
bakerensis	elliptical	7–10 × 4.5–6	hyaline	inamyloid	smooth
camarophyllus	elliptical	7–9 × 4–5	hyaline	inamyloid	smooth
coccineus	elliptical	7–11 × 4–5	hyaline	inamyloid	smooth
conicus	elliptical	8–14 × 5–7	hyaline	inamyloid	smooth
cuspidatus	elliptical	8–12 × 4–6.5	hyaline	inamyloid	smooth
laetus	elliptical	5–8 × 3–5	hyaline	inamyloid	smooth
miniatus	elliptical	6–10 × 4–6	hyaline	inamyloid	smooth
psittacinus	elliptical	8–10 × 4–4.5	hyaline	inamyloid	smooth
var. *californicus*					
psittacinus	elliptical	6.5–8 × 4–5	hyaline	inamyloid	smooth
var. *psittacinus*					
puniceus	elliptical	8–11 × 4–6	hyaline	inamyloid	smooth
roseibrunneus	elliptical	7.5–9 × 3.5–5	hyaline	inamyloid	smooth
spadiceus	elliptical	8–10 × 5–5.5	hyaline	inamyloid	smooth
turundus	elliptical	9–14 × 5–8	hyaline	inamyloid	smooth
Hymenoscyphus fructigenus	spindle-shaped	13–19 × 3–5	hyaline	inamyloid	smooth
Hypomyces chrysospermus	spindle-shaped	25–30 × 5–6	hyaline	inamyloid	smooth
hyalinus	spindle-shaped	13–22 × 4.5–6.5	hyaline	inamyloid	strongly warted
lactifluorum	spindle-shaped	35–50 × 6–8	hyaline	inamyloid	with low, rounded warts
luteovirens	spindle-shaped	28–35 × 4.5–5.5	hyaline	inamyloid	finely warted

GENUS AND SPECIES	SPORE SHAPE	SPORE SIZE (in micrometers)	MICROSCOPIC COLOR	MELZER'S REACTION	SURFACE FEATURES
Hypsizygus tessulatus	globose	5–7	hyaline	inamyloid	smooth
Inocybe caesariata	elliptical	9–12.5 × 5–7	pale brown	inamyloid	smooth
geophylla	elliptical	7.5–11 × 5–7	pale brown	inamyloid	smooth
lilacina	elliptical	7–9 × 4–4.5	pale brown	inamyloid	smooth
olpidiocystis	elliptical	9–12 × 5–6	pale brown	inamyloid	smooth
pudica	elliptical	8–10 × 4.5–6	pale brown	inamyloid	smooth
Ischnoderma resinosum	cylindrical to sausage-shaped	4.5–6.5 × 1.5–2.5	hyaline	inamyloid	smooth
Laccaria amethystina	globose	7–10	hyaline	inamyloid	with spines
amythesteo-occidentalis	subglobose to elliptical	6.5–10.5 × 6.5–9.2	hyaline	inamyloid	with spines
bicolor	oval	6.9–8.7 × 6–7.8	hyaline	inamyloid	with spines
laccata	broadly elliptical to subglobose	7.5–10 × 7–8.5	hyaline	inamyloid	with spines
ochropurpurea	globose	8–10	hyaline	inamyloid	with spines
trullisata	elliptical	16–22 × 6–9	hyaline	inamyloid	slightly roughened
vinaceo-brunnea	subglobose to elliptical	7–10.5 × 6.5–9.7	hyaline	inamyloid	with spines
Lactarius chrysorheus	elliptical	6–9 × 5.5–6.9	hyaline	amyloid	with warts and ridges
corrugis	subglobose	9–12 × 8.5–12	hyaline	amyloid	with warts and ridges
deceptivus	elliptical	9–13 × 7.5–9	hyaline	amyloid	with warts and ridges
deliciosus	oval to globose	8–11 × 7–9	hyaline	amyloid	with warts and ridges
hygrophoroides	elliptical	7.5–10.5 × 6–7.5	hyaline	amyloid	with warts and ridges
indigo	elliptical	7–9 × 5.5–7.5	hyaline	amyloid	with warts and ridges
maculatus	elliptical	9–12 × 7.5–10.5	hyaline	amyloid	with warts and ridges
paradoxus	elliptical	7–9 × 5.5–6.5	pale yellow	amyloid	with warts and ridges
piperatus	elliptical	4.5–7 × 5–5.4	hyaline	amyloid	with warts and ridges
piperatus var. glaucescens	elliptical	6.5–9 × 5.5–6.5	hyaline	amyloid	with warts and ridges
rubrilacteus	elliptical	7.5–9 × 6–7.5	hyaline	amyloid	with warts and ridges
subpalustris	subglobose	8–11 × 7–9	hyaline	amyloid	with warts and ridges
subpurpureus	elliptical	8–11 × 6.5–8	pale yellow	amyloid	with warts and ridges
subvellereus	elliptical	7.5–9 × 6–7	hyaline	amyloid	with warts and ridges
thyinos	oval	9–12 × 7.5–9	hyaline	amyloid	with warts and ridges

Species	Shape	Size	Color	Reaction	Surface
uvidus	subglobose	7.5–9.5 × 6.5–7.5	hyaline	amyloid	with warts and ridges
vellereus	elliptical	7.5–9.5 × 6.5–8.5	hyaline	amyloid	with warts and ridges
vinaceorufescens	elliptical	6.5–9 × 6–7	hyaline	amyloid	with warts and ridges
volemus	subglobose	7.5–10 × 7.5–9	hyaline	amyloid	with warts and ridges
xanthogalactus	elliptical	7–9 × 5.7–6.9	hyaline	amyloid	with warts and ridges
Laetiporus semialbinus	oval to elliptical	5–7 × 3–4.5	hyaline	inamyloid	smooth
sulphureus	oval to elliptical	5–8 × 4–5	hyaline	inamyloid	smooth
Laxitextum bicolor	elliptical to oval	3.5–4.5 × 2–3	hyaline	inamyloid	smooth
Leccinum aurantiacum	elliptical	13–18 × 3.5–5	pale brown	inamyloid	smooth
insigne	elliptical	13–16 × 4–5.5	pale brown	inamyloid	smooth
scabrum	elliptical	15–19 × 5–7	pale brown	inamyloid	smooth
Lentinellus cochleatus	subglobose	3.5–5.5 × 3.5–4.5	hyaline	inamyloid	with minute spines
montanus	oval	4.5–6.5 × 4–5	hyaline	amyloid	with small spines
ursinus	subglobose	3–4.5 × 2–3.5	hyaline	amyloid	minute spines
vulpinus	oval	3.5–4.5 × 2.5–3.5	hyaline	amyloid	with small spines
Lentinus adhaerens	cylindrical	6–10 × 2.5–3.5	hyaline	inamyloid	smooth
kauffmanii	elliptical	5–6 × 2–2.5	hyaline	inamyloid	smooth
Lenzites betulina	cylindrical	4.5–6 × 2–3	hyaline	inamyloid	smooth
Leotia atrovirens	spindle-shaped	16–22 × 4–5	hyaline	inamyloid	smooth
lubrica	slightly spindle-shaped, with rounded ends	20–25 × 5–6	hyaline	inamyloid	smooth, 6- to 8-celled, often slightly curved
viscosa	spindle-shaped	17–26 × 4–6	hyaline	inamyloid	smooth
Lepiota americana	elliptical	8–14 × 5–10	hyaline	dextrinoid	smooth, with apical pore
cristata	bullet-shaped	6.3–8 × 3–4.7	hyaline	dextrinoid	smooth
felina	oval to elliptical	6–7.5 × 3–4	hyaline	dextrinoid	smooth
glabridisca	elliptical	6.3–10 × 4–5.5	hyaline	dextrinoid	smooth
helveola	oval to elliptical	5.8–8 × 3–4.6	hyaline	dextrinoid	smooth
josserandii	elliptical	6–8 × 2–5	hyaline	dextrinoid	smooth
naucinoides	oval	7–9 × 5–6	hyaline	dextrinoid	smooth, with apical pore
procera	oval	12–18 × 8–12	hyaline	dextrinoid	smooth, with apical pore
rachodes	elliptical	6–9.5 × 6–7	hyaline	dextrinoid	smooth
rubrotincta	elliptical	6.3–10 × 4–5.5	hyaline	dextrinoid	smooth
Leucopaxillus albissimus	elliptical	5.5–8.5 × 4–6	hyaline	amyloid	with warts
amarus	globose	3–6	hyaline	amyloid	with warts
Limacella glioderma	globose	3–4	hyaline	inamyloid	smooth
glischra	globose	3–5.5	hyaline	inamyloid	smooth
solidipes	globose	4–5	hyaline	inamyloid	smooth

GENUS AND SPECIES	SPORE SHAPE	SPORE SIZE (in micrometers)	MICROSCOPIC COLOR	MELZER'S REACTION	SURFACE FEATURES
Lycoperdon pyriforme	globose	3–3.5	pale yellow-brown	inamyloid	smooth
perlatum	globose	3.5–4.5	pale brown	inamyloid	with minute spines
Lyophyllum montanum	elliptical	6.5–8 × 3.5–4	hyaline	inamyloid	smooth
Marasmiellus albuscorticis	spindle-shaped	10–15 × 5–6	hyaline	inamyloid	smooth
nigripes	triangular	8–9 × 8–9	hyaline	inamyloid	smooth
Marasmius cohaerens	elliptical	7–10 × 3–6	hyaline	inamyloid	smooth
delectans	elliptical	6–10 × 2.8–5	hyaline	inamyloid	smooth
fulvoferrugineus	elliptical	15–18 × 3–4.5	hyaline	inamyloid	smooth
glabellus	elliptical	7–11.5 × 3–6	hyaline	inamyloid	smooth
nigrodiscus	elliptical	6–7 × 3–4.5	hyaline	inamyloid	smooth
oreades	elliptical	7–11 × 4–7	hyaline	inamyloid	smooth
plicatulus	elliptical	11–15 × 5–6.5	hyaline	inamyloid	smooth
pulcherripes	elliptical	11–16 × 3–4.5	hyaline	inamyloid	smooth
rotula	elliptical	6–10 × 3–5	hyaline	inamyloid	smooth
scorodonius	elliptical	7–10 × 3–5	hyaline	inamyloid	smooth
siccus	elliptical	13–18 × 3–4.5	hyaline	inamyloid	smooth
spissus	elliptical	5.2–8.5 × 2.6–3.4	hyaline	inamyloid	smooth
strictipes	elliptical	6.3–10.5 × 3–4.5	hyaline	inamyloid	smooth
sullivantii	elliptical	7–9 × 3–5.5	hyaline	inamyloid	smooth
Melanoleuca alboflavida	oval	7–9 × 4–5.5	hyaline	amyloid	roughened with warts
graminicola	elliptical	7–9 × 5–6	hyaline	amyloid	with small warts
melaleuca	elliptical	7–8.5 × 5–5.5	hyaline	amyloid	roughened with warts
Meripilus giganteus	elliptical	6–7 × 4.5–6	hyaline	inamyloid	smooth
Morchella elata	elliptical to oval	18–25 × 11–15	hyaline	inamyloid	smooth
esculenta	elliptical	20–24 × 12–24	hyaline	inamyloid	smooth
semilibera	elliptical	24–30 × 12–15	hyaline	inamyloid	smooth
Mutinus caninus	cylindrical	3.5–5 × 1.5–2	hyaline	inamyloid	smooth
elegans	cylindrical	4–7 × 2–3	hyaline	inamyloid	smooth
Mycena abramsii	elliptical	11–13 × 4.5–5.5	hyaline	amyloid	smooth
amabilissima	elliptical	7–9 × 3–4	hyaline	inamyloid	smooth
atkinsoniana	elliptical	7–9 × 4–6	hyaline	amyloid	smooth
fuliginaria	oval	3–4 × 3–4	hyaline	amyloid	smooth
leaiana	elliptical	7–10 × 5–6	hyaline	amyloid	smooth

Species	Shape	Dimensions	Colour	Amyloid	Surface
lilacifolia	elliptical	6–7 × 3–3.5	hyaline	inamyloid	smooth
luteopallens	elliptical	7–9 × 4.5–5	hyaline	amyloid	smooth
monticola	elliptical	7–10 × 4–5	hyaline	inamyloid	smooth
pura	elliptical	5–9 × 3–4	hyaline	amyloid	smooth
roseocandida	elliptical	6–8 × 3–3.5	hyaline	inamyloid	smooth
strobilinoides	elliptical	7–9 × 4–5	hyaline	amyloid	smooth
subincarnata	elliptical	7–10 × 4–5	hyaline	inamyloid	smooth
taxodii	oval	4–6 × 3–4	hyaline	amyloid	smooth
Naematoloma capnoides	elliptical	6–7.5 × 3.5–4.5	pale brown	inamyloid	smooth, with apical pore
fasciculare	elliptical	6.5–8 × 3.5–4	pale purple-brown	inamyloid	smooth, with apical pore
sublateritium	elliptical	6–7.5 × 3.5–4	pale purple-brown	inamyloid	smooth, with apical pore
Nidula candida	elliptical	8–10 × 4–6	hyaline	inamyloid	smooth
niveo-tomentosa	subglobose to elliptical	6–9 × 5–6	hyaline	inamyloid	smooth
Nidularia pulvinata	oval to short-elliptical	6–10 × 4–7	hyaline	inamyloid	smooth
Nivatogastrium nubigenum	elliptical	7.5–9 × 5.5–6.5	pale brown	inamyloid	smooth, with apical pore and short peg
Omphalotus olearius	globose or subglobose	3.5–5 × 3.5–5	hyaline	inamyloid	smooth
olivascens	globose or subglobose	3.5–5 × 3.5–5	hyaline	inamyloid	smooth
Oudemansiella longipes	oval	8–9 × 6–6.5	hyaline	inamyloid	smooth
radicata	elliptical	14–17 × 9–11	hyaline	inamyloid	smooth
Panaeolus campanulatus	elliptical	13–16 × 8–11	purple-black	inamyloid	smooth, with apical pore
foenisecii	elliptical	11–18 × 6–9	purple-black	inamyloid	roughened, with apical pore
subbalteatus	elliptical	11–14 × 7–9	purple-black	inamyloid	smooth, with apical pore
Panellus serotinus	sausage-shaped	4.5–5.5 × 1.5–2	hyaline	amyloid	smooth
stipticus	sausage-shaped	3–6 × 2–3	hyaline	amyloid	smooth
Panus rudis	elliptical	4.5–7 × 2.5–3	hyaline	dextrinoid	smooth
Paxillus atrotomentosus	oval	5–7 × 3–4	pale yellow	inamyloid	smooth
involutus	elliptical	7–9 × 4–6	pale yellow	inamyloid	smooth
Phaeocollybia kauffmanii	almond-shaped	8–11 × 4.5–7	pale brown	inamyloid	minutely roughened
Phallus impudicus	elliptical	3–3.7 × 1.3–2	pale yellow-brown	inamyloid	smooth
ravenelii	cylindrical	3–4 × 1–1.5	hyaline	inamyloid	smooth
Phlebia radiata	sausage-shaped	3.5–4.5 × 1.5–2	hyaline	inamyloid	smooth, with a pointed tip
tremellosa	sausage-shaped	3–3.5 × 0.5–1	hyaline	inamyloid	smooth
Phlogiotis helvelloides	elliptical	9–12 × 4–6	hyaline	inamyloid	smooth
Pholiota albocrenulata	elliptical	10–18 × 6–8	yellow-brown	inamyloid	smooth, with apical pore
aurivella	elliptical	7–10 × 4.5–6	pale brown	inamyloid	smooth, with apical pore

153

GENUS AND SPECIES	SPORE SHAPE	SPORE SIZE (in micrometers)	MICROSCOPIC COLOR	MELZER'S REACTION	SURFACE FEATURES
Pholiota destruens	elliptical	7–9.5 × 4–4.5	yellow-brown	inamyloid	smooth, with apical pore
flammans	elliptical	4–5 × 2.5–3	pale brown	inamyloid	smooth
malicola	elliptical	7.5–11 × 4.5–5.5	pale brown	inamyloid	smooth, with apical pore
var. *macropoda*					
malicola var. *malicola*	elliptical	8.5–12 × 4.5–6	pale brown	inamyloid	smooth, with apical pore
squarrosa	elliptical	5–8 × 3.5–4.5	pale brown	inamyloid	smooth, with apical pore
squarrosoides	elliptical	4–6 × 2.5–3.5	pale brown	inamyloid	smooth
Phyllotopsis nidulans	sausage-shaped	5–7 × 2–2.5	hyaline	inamyloid	smooth
Piptoporus betulinus	sausage-shaped	5–6 × 1–1.5	hyaline	inamyloid	smooth
Pisolithus tinctorius	globose	7–12	pale brown	inamyloid	with spines
Pleurocybella porrigens	oval to globose	5–7 × 4.5–6.5	hyaline	inamyloid	smooth
Pleurotus dryinus	elliptical	9–12 × 3.5–4	hyaline	inamyloid	smooth
ostreatus	elliptical	8–12 × 3.5–4.5	hyaline	inamyloid	smooth
Plicaturopsis crispa	cylindrical	3–4 × 1–1.5	hyaline	inamyloid	smooth
Pluteus admirabilis	elliptical	5.5–7 × 4.5–6	hyaline	inamyloid	smooth
atromarginatus	elliptical	6.5–8 × 4–5	hyaline	inamyloid	smooth
aurantiorugosus	elliptical	6–7 × 4.5–5.5	hyaline	inamyloid	smooth
cervinus	elliptical	5.5–7 × 4–5	hyaline	inamyloid	smooth
flavofuligineus	elliptical	6–7 × 4.5–5.5	hyaline	inamyloid	smooth
magnus	elliptical	6–8 × 4–6	hyaline	inamyloid	smooth
pellitus	elliptical	7–8 × 5–6	hyaline	inamyloid	smooth
petasatus	elliptical	6–7.5 × 4.5–5	hyaline	inamyloid	smooth
Polyozellus multiplex	globose	4–6	hyaline	inamyloid	with large warts
Polyporus arcularius	cylindrical	7–11 × 2–3	hyaline	inamyloid	smooth
brumalis	sausage-shaped	5–7 × 2–2.5	hyaline	inamyloid	smooth
squamosus	elliptical	10–16 × 4–6	hyaline	inamyloid	smooth
umbellatus	cylindrical	8–10 × 2.5–3.5	hyaline	inamyloid	smooth
Psathyrella delineata	elliptical	6.5–8 × 4.5–5.5	brown	inamyloid	smooth, with apical pore
hydrophila	elliptical	4.5–6 × 3–3.5	brown	inamyloid	smooth, with apical pore
rugocephala	elliptical	9–11 × 6–7.5	brown	inamyloid	warted, with apical pore
septentrionalis	elliptical	7–10 × 4.5–5	pale brown	inamyloid	smooth, with apical pore
velutina	elliptical	9–12 × 6–8	pale brown	inamyloid	smooth, with apical pore
Pseudohydnum gelatinosum	globose	5–7	hyaline	inamyloid	smooth

154

Species	Shape	Size	Color	Reaction	Ornamentation
Pseudoplectania nigrella	globose	12–14	hyaline	inamyloid	smooth
Psilocybe coprophila	elliptical	11–14 × 7–8.5	dark brown	inamyloid	smooth, with apical pore
cubensis	oval to short-elliptical	10–17 × 7–10	dark brown	inamyloid	smooth, with apical pore
Pulveroboletus ravenelii	elliptical	8–10.5 × 4–5	pale yellow	inamyloid	smooth
Pycnoporus cinnabarinus	cylindrical	5–6 × 2–2.5	hyaline	inamyloid	smooth
sanguineus	oval	4–5 × 2–3	hyaline	inamyloid	smooth
Ramaria araiospora	cylindrical	8–13 × 3–4.5	hyaline	inamyloid	finely roughened
botrytis	elliptical	11–17 × 4–6	hyaline	inamyloid	smooth, longitudinally striate
formosa	elliptical	9–12 × 4.5–6	hyaline	inamyloid	with small warts
Ramariopsis kunzii	oval to globose	3–5.5 × 2.5–4.5	hyaline	inamyloid	minutely roughened
Rhodotus palmatus	globose	4.5–7	hyaline	inamyloid	with warts
Rozites caperata	almond-shaped	11–14 × 7–9	pale yellow	inamyloid	slightly roughened
Russula bevipes	elliptical	8–11 × 6.5–10	hyaline	amyloid	warts and ridges
claroflava	subglobose	8–11 × 7.5–9	hyaline	amyloid	warts and ridges
compacta	elliptical	7.5–10 × 6–8.5	hyaline	amyloid	warts and ridges
emetica	elliptical	8–11 × 6.5–9	hyaline	amyloid	warts and ridges
fragrantissima	subglobose	7.5–10 × 6.5–9.5	hyaline	amyloid	warts and ridges
granulata	subglobose	6–8 × 5–6	hyaline	amyloid	warts and ridges
laurocerasi	subglobose	7–10.5 × 7.9	hyaline	amyloid	warts and ridges
pectinatoides	subglobose	6–9 × 5–7	hyaline	amyloid	warts and ridges
pulverulenta	short-elliptical	6–8 × 5–6.8	hyaline	amyloid	warts and ridges
silvicola	subglobose	6–10 × 6–9	hyaline	amyloid	warts and ridges
Sarcoscypha coccinea	elliptical	24–40 × 12–14	hyaline	inamyloid	smooth
occidentalis	elliptical	20–22 × 10–12	hyaline	inamyloid	smooth
Schizophyllum commune	cylindrical	3–4 × 1–1.5	hyaline	inamyloid	smooth
Scleroderma areolatum	globose	9–14	pale brown	inamyloid	with spines
citrinum	globose	8–13	pale brown	inamyloid	minute spines and net-like ridges
Scutellinia scutellata	elliptical	18–19 × 10–12	hyaline	inamyloid	minutely roughened
Sebacina concrescens	oval to cylindrical	9–14 × 5–7	hyaline	inamyloid	smooth
Sparassis crispa	oval	5–6.5 × 3–3.5	hyaline	inamyloid	smooth
spathulata	oval	4–7 × 3–4	hyaline	inamyloid	smooth
Stereum hirsutum	cylindrical	5–8 × 2–3.5	hyaline	inamyloid	smooth
ostrea	cylindrical	5.5–7.5 × 2–3	hyaline	inamyloid	smooth
striatum	cylindrical	6–8.5 × 2–3.5	hyaline	inamyloid	smooth
Strobilomyces confusus	oval	10.5–12.5 × 9.7–10.2	grayish black	inamyloid	roughened or with ridges

GENUS AND SPECIES	SPORE SHAPE	SPORE SIZE (in micrometers)	MICROSCOPIC COLOR	MELZER'S REACTION	SURFACE FEATURES
Strobilomyces dryophilus	oval	9.5–12 × 7.5–9	grayish black	inamyloid	roughened, with net-like ridges
floccopus	globose to oval	9–16 × 8–12	grayish black	inamyloid	roughened, with net-like ridges
Stropharia ambigua	elliptical	11–14 × 6–7.5	dark brown	inamyloid	smooth, with apical pore
coronilla	elliptical	7–10 × 4–6	pale brownish black	inamyloid	smooth, with apical pore
hardii	elliptical	5–9 × 3–5	pale brown	inamyloid	smooth, with apical pore
hornemannii	elliptical	10.5–13 × 5.5–7	grayish brown	inamyloid	smooth, with apical pore
rugosoannulata	elliptical	10–13 × 7.5–9	grayish black	inamyloid	smooth, with apical pore
squamosa var. *squamosa*	elliptical	12–14 × 6–7.5	brown	inamyloid	smooth, with apical pore
squamosa var. *thrausta*	elliptical	12–13.5 × 6–7	brown	inamyloid	smooth, with off-center apical pore
Suillus caerulescens	elliptical	8–11 × 3–5	pale brown	inamyloid	smooth
cavipes	elliptical	7–10 × 3.5–4	pale brown	inamyloid	smooth
decipiens	elliptical	9–10 × 3–4	pale brown	inamyloid	smooth
granulatus	elliptical	7–10 × 2.5–3.5	pale brown	inamyloid	smooth
grevillei	elliptical	8–11 × 3–4	pale brown	inamyloid	smooth
lakei	elliptical	7–10 × 3–4	pale brown	inamyloid	smooth
luteus	elliptical	6–11 × 2.5–4	pale brown	inamyloid	smooth
pictus	elliptical	8–12 × 3.5–5	pale brown	inamyloid	smooth
ponderosus	elliptical	8–12 × 3.5–5	pale brown	inamyloid	smooth
subluteus	elliptical	6–11 × 2–4	pale brown	inamyloid	smooth
Syzygospora mycetophila	oval to elliptical	2–4 × 1.5–2.5	hyaline	inamyloid	smooth
Tremella fuciformis	elliptical	6–11 × 5–8.5	hyaline	inamyloid	smooth
lutescens	oval	10–16 × 8–12	hyaline	inamyloid	smooth
mesenterica	elliptical	7–15 × 6–10	hyaline	inamyloid	smooth
reticulata	globose to sausage-shaped	9–11 × 5–6	hyaline	inamyloid	smooth
Trichaptum abietinus	cylindrical	4–6 × 1.5–2.5	hyaline	inamyloid	smooth
biformis	cylindrical	5–6.5 × 2–2.5	hyaline	inamyloid	smooth
Tricholoma magnivelare	elliptical	5–7 × 4.5–5.5	hyaline	inamyloid	smooth
Tricholomopsis platyphylla	oval	7–9 × 5–7	hyaline	inamyloid	smooth
Tylopilus felleus	elliptical	9–15 × 3–5	hyaline	inamyloid	smooth
indecisus	cylindrical	10–13 × 3–4	hyaline	inamyloid	smooth

Species	Spore shape	Spore size	Color	Reaction	Surface
plumbeoviolaceus	elliptical	9–13 × 3–4	hyaline	inamyloid	smooth
rubrobrunneus	elliptical	8–14 × 3–4.5	hyaline	dextrinoid	smooth
Verpa bohemica	elliptical	60–80 × 15–18	hyaline	inamyloid	smooth
conica	elliptical	22–26 × 12–16	hyaline	inamyloid	smooth
Volvariella bombycina	elliptical	6.5–10.5 × 4.5–6.5	hyaline	inamyloid	smooth
hypopithys	oval	5.4–9.9 × 3.3–6	hyaline	inamyloid	smooth
pusilla	elliptical	5.5–8.5 × 4–6	hyaline	inamyloid	smooth
speciosa	elliptical	11.2–21 × 7–12.5	hyaline	inamyloid	smooth
surrecta	elliptical	5.5–7.5 × 3–4	hyaline	inamyloid	smooth
Wynnea americana	elliptical	32–40 × 15–16	hyaline	inamyloid	pointed at each end, longitudinally striate
sparassoides	elliptical	32–36 × 12–15	hyaline	inamyloid	longitudinal ridges
Xeromphalina campanella	elliptical	5–9 × 3–4	hyaline	amyloid	smooth
cauticinalis	elliptical	4–7 × 2.5–3.5	hyaline	amyloid	smooth
kauffmanii	elliptical	5–6 × 3–3.5	hyaline	amyloid	smooth
Xylaria hypoxylon	bean-shaped	11–14 × 5–6	pale grayish black	inamyloid	smooth
polymorpha	spindle-shaped	20–30 × 5–10	pale brownish black	inamyloid	smooth, 1 side flattened
Xylobus frustulatus	oval	3.5–5 × 2.5–3	hyaline	inamyloid	smooth

157

Further Reading

Mushroom Terminology and Nomenclature

Hawksworth, D. L., B. C. Sutton, and G. C. Ainsworth. *Dictionary of the Fungi.* Kew, Surrey: Commonwealth Mycological Institute, 1983. Comprehensive work on mycological terminology, with emphasis on nomenclature; black-and-white line drawings.

Largent, D. L. *How to Identify Mushrooms to Genus I: Macroscopic Features* [rev. ed.]. Eureka, Calif.: Mad River Press, 1986. Detailed account of macroscopic mushroom features and stature types; keys to genera; numerous line drawings.

Largent, D. L., D. Johnson, and R. Watling. *How to Identify Mushrooms to Genus III: Microscopic Features.* Eureka, Calif.: Mad River Press, 1977. Detailed survey of microscopic features; numerous drawings and black-and-white photographs.

Miller, O. K., Jr., and D. F. Farr. *An Index of the Common Fungi of North America (Synonymy and Common Names).* Vaduz, Liechtenstein: J. Cramer. Bibliotheca Mycologica 44, 1975. Extensive species list with both scientific and common names; no illustrations.

Snell, W. H., and E. A. Dick. *A Glossary of Mycology.* Cambridge, Mass.: Harvard U. Press, 1957. Definitions of nearly 7,000 terms, many related to mushrooms; 31 pages of line drawings.

Identification Guides

Arora, D. *Mushrooms Demystified: A Comprehensive Guide to the Fleshy Fungi,* 2d ed. Berkeley, Calif.: Ten Speed Press, 1986. Keys to over 2,000 species, many supplemented with short descriptions; over 800 photographs (over 200 in color); second edition expanded to cover the entire U.S.A.

Dickinson, C., and J. Lucas. *The Encyclopedia of Mushrooms.* New York: Putnam, 1979. Descriptions of over 400 species, most accompanied by color photographs or sketches; some line drawings; extensive introduction on the biology of mushrooms and related topics.

Groves, J. W. *Edible and Poisonous Mushrooms of Canada* [2d rev. ed.]. Ottawa: Research Branch, Agriculture Canada, 1979 [publication #A43-1112/1979E]. Keys and descriptions; many small color photographs.

Largent, D. L., and H. D. Thiers. *How to Identify Mushrooms to Genus II: Field Identification of Genera.* Eureka, Calif.: Mad River Press, 1977. Summaries of field characters of mushroom genera; no illustrations.

Lincoff, G. H. *The Audubon Society Field Guide to North American Mushrooms.* New York: Knopf, 1981. Color photographs and descriptions of over 700 species, with short comments on several hundred more.

Miller, O. K., Jr. *Mushrooms of North America.* New York: Dutton, 1979. Keys and descriptions of 422 species, with 292 color photographs.

Smith, A. H. *A Field Guide to Western Mushrooms.* Ann Arbor, Mich.; U. of Michigan Press, 1975. Keys, color photographs, and descriptions of 201 western species.

Smith, A. H., H. V. Smith, and N. S. Weber. *How to Know the Gilled Mushrooms.* Dubuque, Iowa: William C. Brown, 1979. Keys, descriptions, and 453 black-and-white sketches; covers over 800 species.

Smith, A. H., H. V. Smith, and N. S. Weber. *How to Know the Non-gilled Mushrooms,* 2d ed. Dubuque, Iowa: William C. Brown, 1981. Keys, descriptions, and 340 black-and-white sketches.

Smith, A. H., and N. S. Weber. *The Mushroom Hunter's Field Guide.* Ann Arbor, Mich.: U. of Michigan Press, 1980. Keys, color photographs, and descriptions of 282 species.

Weber, N. S., and A. H. Smith. *A Field Guide to Southern Mushrooms.* Ann Arbor, Mich.: U. of Michigan Press, 1985. Keys, color photographs, and descriptions of 240 southern species.

Mushroom Poisioning

Ammirati, J. F., J. A. Traquir, and P. A. Horgen. *Poisonous Mushrooms of the Northern United States and Canada.* Minneapolis: U. of Minnesota Press, 1985. Recommended for advanced amateurs; many excellent color photographs and black-and-white line drawings accompanying detailed descriptions of species, with a summary of symptoms of various types of mushroom poisoning.

Hanrahan, J. P., and M. A. Gordon. "Mushroom Poisoning: Case Reports and a Review of Therapy." *Journal of the American Medical Association,* 251 (1984): 1057-1061. A presentation of current therapeutic approaches. See also letters in reply, JAMA 252 (1984): 1685, 3130; 253 (1985): 3252.

Lincoff, G. H., and D. H. Mitchell. *Toxic and Hallucinogenic Mushroom Poisoning.* New York: Van Nostrand Reinhold, 1977. For advanced amateurs, with many color photographs and a detailed discussion of aspects of mushroom poisoning—symptoms, treatments, etc.

Glossary

See also the illustrated glossary in the front of the book and the Checklist of Field Characters.

Amyloid—staining grayish to blue-black in Melzer's reagent.

Apical pore—a small opening or thin area in the wall at one end (the apex) of a spore. Also known as germ pore.

Apiculus—a short projection at or near one end (the base) of a spore; the attachment point of the spore.

Appendiculate—describes a mushroom cap edge that is adorned or fringed with the fragmented remnants of the partial veil.

Ascus (plural, asci)—a sac-like cell in which ascospores (usually eight) are formed; characteristic of sac fungi (Ascomycetes).

Ascospore—a spore formed within an ascus.

Basidiospore—a spore formed on a basidium.

Basidium (plural, basidia)—a variously shaped, but typically club-shaped, cell on which basidiospores (usually four) are formed; characteristic of club fungi (Basidiomycetes).

Button—a young, unexpanded, but fully formed mushroom (all parts present).

Conifer—a cone-bearing tree, such as pine or juniper, with needle-like or scale-like leaves (*compare* HARDWOOD).

Decurrent—descending or running down the stalk (describes one form of attachment of mushroom gills to the stalk).

Dextrinoid (pseudoamyloid)—staining orange to orange-brown or pinkish red to dark red to reddish brown in Melzer's reagent.

Fibril—a thread-like to hair-like structure present on the cap or stalk of some mushrooms.

Fusoid—spindle-shaped; tapering to a point at both ends.

Globose—round.

Hardwood—a flowering tree, such as oak or beech, with broad leaves (*compare* CONIFER).

Hyaline—transparent; clear and nearly colorless.

Inamyloid—not amyloid and not dextrinoid; unchanging or pale yellow in Melzer's reagent.

Latex—a watery to milk-like fluid that exudes from some mushrooms when they are cut or broken.

Melzer's reagent—a special solution containing iodine, used to test fungal spores for color reaction.

Mycorrhizal association—an intimate physical and physiological association between a fungus and the rootlets of a tree, of mutual nutritional benefit to both.

Parasite—an organism that lives on or in another organism and at the nutritional expense of the other organism.

Partial Veil—a layer of tissue that connects the stalk to the edge of the cap (enclosing the gills) in some mushrooms when young; upon cap expansion in maturing specimens, usually forms a ring on the stalk or an appendiculate cap edge or both.

Pore—a small, circular to angular opening.

Reticulum—a system of raised, net-like ridges; found on the surface of the stalk or spores of some mushrooms.

Rhizomorph—a group of thick, rope-like strands of hyphae growing together as a single organized unit.

Rimose—describes a mushroom cap edge that is cracked or split from the edge toward the center.

Sclerotium (plural, sclerotia)—a small, spherical to irregular body composed of resting hyphae; under proper conditions it can germinate to form active hyphae or fruiting bodies.

Septate—divided by crosswalls.

Striate—having small, more or less parallel lines or furrows.

Subfusoid—somewhat spindle-shaped; tapering slightly at both ends.

Subglobose—nearly round.

Truncate—appearing cut off or chopped off at the end.

Universal Veil—a covering layer of tissue that completely envelopes some mushrooms when young; upon stalk elongation and cap expansion in maturing specimens, forms a fragmented or intact cup at the base of the stalk and often also forms superficial fragmented scales or patches on the cap surface.

Warts—small, raised, regular to irregularly shaped bumps on the surface of a spore or a mushroom cap; when on the cap, sometimes formed by pieces of tissue remaining after disintegration of the universal veil.

Index of Species

Entries give species name first and genus second. Page references in boldface refer to species descriptions accompanied by a photograph.

165

Index of Genera

Index of Common Names

Entries include only those species that are illustrated with photographs.

Credits

Other books in the authoritative, highly popular
Macmillan Field Guide Series
are available at your local bookstore or by mail.
To order directly, return the coupon below to

MACMILLAN PUBLISHING COMPANY
Special Sales Department
866 Third Avenue
New York, New York 10022

Line Sequence	ISBN	Author/Title	Price	Quantity
1	0020796501	Dunlop: **ASTRONOMY,** paperback	$ 8.95	_____
2	002063370X	Moody: **FOSSILS,** paperback	$ 8.95	_____
3	0020796404	Bell/Wright: **ROCKS AND MINERALS,** paperback	$ 8.95	_____
4	0020796609	Bull: **BIRDS OF NORTH AMERICA,** paperback	$ 9.95	_____
5	0025182307	Bull: **BIRDS OF NORTH AMERICA,** hardcover	$19.95	_____
6	002063420X	Mohlenbrock: **WILDFLOWERS,** paperback	$ 9.95	_____
7	0025854402	Mohlenbrock: **WILDFLOWERS,** hardcover	$24.95	_____
8	0020137001	Dunlop: **WEATHER AND FORECASTING,** paperback	$ 8.95	_____
9	0020636903	Bessette/Sundberg: **MUSHROOMS,** paperback	$12.95	_____
10	0026152606	Bessette/Sundberg: **MUSHROOMS,** hardcover	$24.95	_____
11	0020634307	Mohlenbrock/Thieret: **TREES,** paperback	$12.95	_____
12	0025854607	Mohlenbrock/Thieret: **TREES,** hardcover	$24.95	_____
			Sub-total $	_____

Please add postage and handling costs—$1.00 for the first book
and 50¢ for each additional book $ _____

Total $ _____

_____ Enclosed is my check/money order payable to Macmillan Publishing Co.

_____ Bill my _____ MasterCard _____ Visa Card # _____

Expiration date _____ Signature _____

—Charge orders valid only with
signature

Control No. [   ]   Order Type [Reg]   Lines [   ]   Units

Ship to:_____   Bill to:_____

_____   _____

_____   _____

_____Zip Code   _____Zip Code

For information regarding bulk purchases, please write to Special Sales
Director at the above address. Publisher's prices are subject to change without
notice. Offer good May 1, 1987, through December 31, 1988. Allow 3 weeks for
delivery.   FC# 611

About the Authors

Alan Bessette is Associate Professor of Biology and Medical Technology at Utica College of Syracuse University. He received a B.S. in medical technology from the University of Vermont, an M.S. in microbiology from the University of Oregon, and a Ph.D. in mycology from the University of Maine. He teaches microbiology, parasitology, and mycology and conducts research in mycology, with special emphasis on fungal and lichen morphology and taxonomy. Dr. Bessette is a naturalist for the Appalachian and Adirondack Mountain Clubs and an advisor to the Mid York Mycological Society. He conducts many workshops and lectures on the identification of edible and poisonous mushrooms.

Walter J. Sundberg is Associate Professor of Botany at Southern Illinois University at Carbondale. He holds a B.A. and an M.A. in biology from San Francisco State University and a Ph.D. in botany from the University of California at Davis. In addition to teaching mycology, forest pathology, microtechnique, and general biology classes, he conducts a research program on the taxonomy and ultrastructural cytology of fleshy fungi. He has collected mushrooms in many parts of the country over the past 15 years. Dr. Sundberg also conducts mushroom identification workshops, lectures to mushroom clubs and other groups, and acts as a mushroom identification consultant for the regional poison control center. Using fungi as a tool for teaching biological principles in the high school laboratory, Dr. Sundberg is also active in in-service education for high school science teachers.

OUTLINE OF MAJOR GROUPS

Bird's Nest Fungi: Small; cup-shaped or goblet-shaped, resembling a nest with minute, flattened eggs inside. *Page 2.*

Cup and Disc Fungi: Cup-shaped or disc-shaped; inner (upper) surface smooth; outer (lower) surface smooth, downy, or hairy. *Pages 4–6.*

Stinkhorns: Bearing a slimy, foul-smelling spore mass *(a)* at apex of a spongy stalk; or *(b)* lining the inside of stalked or stalkless, outwardly flaring, tapered, finger-like branches; or *(c)* lining the inside of a stalked or stalkless, bird-cage-like sphere. *Page 8.*

Coral and Similar Fungi: Soft and fleshy; upright, without a cap; *(a)* unbranched and cylindrical to club-shaped, or *(b)* branched and coral-like. *Pages 10–12.*

Morels and Similar Fungi: Soft and fleshy; with a distinct stalk and cap; cap ball-like, saddle-like, brain-like, or with numerous pits and ridges. *Pages 14–16.*

Puffballs and Allies: Sac-like; distinct stalk and cap absent; spores borne inside and often powdery. *Pages 18–20.*

Jelly and Jelly-like Fungi: Gelatinous to rubbery when moist; cushion-shaped, ear-shaped, or brain-like; distinct stalk and cap absent; without gills, spines, or pores. *Pages 22–24.*

Smooth and Crust Fungi: Bracket-like, irregularly lobed, or crust-like; on wood or rarely on soil. *Page 26.*

Spine Fungi: With spines (downwardly directed teeth) hanging from the undersurface of a cap, from the undersides or ends of branches of the fruiting body, or from a solid fist-like mass of tissue. *Pages 28–30.*

Polypores and Allies: With pores (the openings of small, downwardly directed tubes) rather than gills; texture tough, leathery to woody; not readily decaying; with or without a stalk; usually on wood. *Pages 32–36.*

Boletes: Cap with pores (rather than gills) on the undersurface; texture soft and fleshy; readily decaying; always with a stalk; on the ground. *Pages 38–46.*

Chanterelles and Similar Fungi: Soft and fleshy; with a distinct stalk and cap; cap expanded and mushroom-like; undersurface may be smooth, slightly wrinkled, minutely bumpy (feeling like sandpaper), or with very thick, shallow, fold-like gills with blunt edges. *Pages 48–52.*

Stalkless and Lateral-stalked Fungi: Cap with thin, blade-like gills on the undersurface; either without a stalk or with a stalk that is distinctly lateral (attached at or very near the cap side). *Pages 54–58.*